BYE BYE BLACK SHIRT!

THE FIGHT AGAINST OSWALD MOSLEY, ANTISEMITISM, AND THE BRITISH UNION OF FASCISTS; 1934–1936

MARK KRANTZ

b

Bookmarks
Publications

About the author

Mark Krantz's previous works include, *The 1842 General Strike* (Bookmarks, 2014) and *The Cotton Famine: Lancashire Textile Workers and the American Civil War* (Red Roof, 2017). He lives in Manchester and is a member of the Socialist Workers Party.

Acknowledgements

Writing this book was only possible with the help and encouragement of many people. Thanks to staff at the People's History Museum. It was their archive collection of cuttings on anti-fascism that first inspired me to write this account of the fight against Mosley's Blackshirts. Thanks to Martin Empson, Rhetta Moran, Donny Gluckstein, Sue Caldwell, Anna Gluckstein, Colm Bryce, Camilla Royle and Mark L. Thomas for their suggestions, advice and support. I am responsible for the final text.

Dedication

This book is dedicated to Julie Waterson[1], inspirational anti-fascist fighter and organiser of the Anti Nazi League. Writing about resistance to fascism in the 1930s, she said it was two key years of mass protests that held back Mosley and the BUF. This book is a history of those struggles.

Bye Bye Blackshirt! The Fight Against Oswald Mosley, Antisemitism, and the British Union of Fascists, 1934-1936
By Mark Krantz

Published 2026 by Bookmarks Publications
c/o 1 Bloomsbury Street, London WC1B 3QE
© Bookmarks Publications • bookmarksbookshop.co.uk

Typeset in Adobe Caslon Pro and Whitney by Ben Windsor.
Printed by Halstan, Amersham HP6 6HJ.

ISBN
Paperback: 978-1-914143-79-3
Kindle : 978-1-914143-80-9
Epub: 978-1-914143-81-6
PDF: 978-1-914143-82-3

Oswald Mosley was heckled at his first public meeting in Manchester when he spoke at a mass fascist rally at the Kings Hall in 1933.

Evelyn Taylor was in the balcony. She was 22 years old and a factory worker. Evelyn stood up and started to shout and heckle the fascist Mosley. He was outraged. To be heckled! And by a woman! The fight against the British Union of Fascists was on.

Over the next three years in Manchester and across the country mass protests held back Mosley and his fascist thugs.

Contents

1 **Foreword**

3 **Introduction**

Chapter 1
12 **Fascist forces grow across Europe**

Chapter 2
21 **Jewish immigration and antisemitism**

Chapter 3
31 **Building mass opposition to Mosley and the BUF: the Manchester example**

Chapter 4
37 **Communists, the Russian Revolution and the United Front**

Chapter 5
45 **1934: the fightback against Mosley begins**

Chapter 6
64 **Halting the fascist momentum**

Chapter 7
78 **Blackshirt Bye Bye**

Chapter 8
84 **Anti-fascists after Cable Street**

94 Bibliography

101 Endnotes

Foreword

A fascist headquarters on the next street! When I lived in Higher Broughton in Salford in the late 1970s, I was shocked to find out that Oswald Mosley once had a headquarters on the street next to ours. The northern headquarters[2] of the British Union of Fascists (BUF) was at 17 Northumberland Street.[3] How could this be? I was full of questions: What did the fascists do there? Who supported them? Who opposed them? Imagine, what if I had been alive then? I knew about Oswald Mosley, Britain's 'would-be' fascist leader. And I knew that Mosley was stopped at the famous Battle of Cable Street in 1936 in the East End of London.[4] "Your grandad was there" at Cable Street, I was told when I was growing up. I was doubtful about this. So, I asked my mum again, "Was grandad really at Cable Street?", "Of course, the whole of the East End was there", she reassured me. "He was throwing dustbins at Mosley's people." As my mother's family lived on the Mile End Road in the East End, I figured my grandad must have indeed been there along with everyone else.

When Hitler bombed London in the Blitz the family home was destroyed, and they had to move to Northampton, a small town in the Midlands. I was born there and brought up as part of a small Jewish community. As a teenager I went to the synagogue and took part in the religious services. I will never forget how at family weddings I saw old relatives with tattooed numbers on their arms. I asked about this. Finding out what happened in the Holocaust, I was devastated. I felt sick in my stomach. I still do today. As a teenager I had so many questions. How could it have happened?

Why did it happen? Why weren't Hitler and the fascists

stopped? And a question I found the hardest to ask: Did Jews like us not fight back?[5] These questions still need answering today.

That is why I have written this book; *Bye Bye Blackshirt: The Fight Against Oswald Mosley, Antisemitism, and the British Union of Fascists, 1934-36*.[6] It is a history of the first anti-fascist movement in Britain, the story of the organised opposition to Britain's first significant fascist party, the BUF. An account of how over "two years the anti-fascist movement successfully held Mosley and the BUF back by mass protests".[7] The opposition to Mosley took place right across the country; from Newcastle to Plymouth, Hull to Liverpool, in Scotland and in Wales.

In Manchester opposition to Mosley and the BUF was organised by young communists who met on Herbert Street, Hightown, in the Cheetham Hill area of the city.[8] The Young Communist League (YCL)[9] members met in a room above a garage. They called themselves the Challenge Club after the *Socialist Challenge* newspaper they sold. Their struggle against Mosley in Manchester is told as part of a wider history of the organised protests against fascism that took place between early 1934 and late 1936. What follows is a history of the rise of fascism and how in Britain it was defeated by mass movements from below, led by young, radical communists in the 1930s.

Introduction

The united front against fascism

Living in Salford I became involved with the Anti Nazi League (ANL) in the late 1970s and read the political writings of Leon Trotsky on how to fight fascism, *Trotsky: Fascism, Stalinism and the United Front 1930-1934*,[10] a publication that "helped educate and train a new generation of revolutionaries in the why's and how's of fighting fascism".[11]

The ANL was an anti-fascist organisation that mobilised thousands of people to oppose the National Front (NF).[12] The NF was founded in 1967 by former BUF member A.K. Chesterton. Leading NF members Martin Webster and John Tyndall had been among the fascist speakers at Mosley's post war meetings.[13] In the 1970s the NF started to gain a lot of support.[14] At the ballot box Webster, the NF national organiser, won 16 percent of the vote in the 1973 West Bromwich by-election.[15] On the streets the NF were "terrorising black communities, openly assaulting black people and 'Reds', and breaking up meetings not just of socialists but of liberals".[16]

To organise opposition to the NF the ANL was set up and operated using a political tactic – the united front.[17] What is the united front and why is it needed? The united front was first consciously developed by revolutionary socialists at an international conference organised to debate political strategies in 1921 in the face of the defeat of the initial revolutionary wave across Europe that followed the Russian Revolution.[18]

In 1923 the distinctive nature of the fascist threat and the need for a united front against fascism was explained by the German communist Clara Zetkin:

Fascism does not enquire whether the factory worker owes his allegiance to the white and blue of Bavaria, to the black, red and gold of the bourgeois Republic, or to the red flag with the hammer and sickle… It is enough that fascism sees the class conscious proletarian in front of it; it strikes him down regardless.

Fascists pose a physical threat to workers, regardless of political colour, belief in royalty, sexuality or gender, union affiliation or religious creed:

> The workers must therefore make common cause in the struggle, without distinction of party or trade union organisation. The self-defence of the proletariat against fascism is one of the strongest factors making for organisation and consolidation of the proletarian united front.[19]

The Russian revolutionary Leon Trotsky explained how fascism is "not merely a system of reprisals, of brute force and of police terror".

> Fascism is a particular governmental system based on the uprooting of all elements of proletarian democracy within bourgeois society… To this end the physical annihilation of the most revolutionary section of the workers does not suffice. It is also necessary to smash all independent and voluntary organisations, to demolish all the defensive bulwarks of the proletariat.[20]

Fascism was not just another right-wing political force. Fascism posed an existential threat to all workers and all working class organisation. Therefore, making common cause against the fascists is a necessity. It requires working together with other political forces – in spite of political differences.

In the early 1930s, as Hitler started to gain mass support, Trotsky called for Germany's Communists and Social Democrats to join forces against their common enemy, but they were divided and unwilling to unite and fight against Hitler's fascists. Tragically, and foreseen by Trotsky, Hitler and the Nazis came to state power in Germany in 1933, just as earlier, Mussolini and his Blackshirts had in Italy in 1922.

Inspired by these fascist victories, Mosley set up the BUF in Britain. From its foundation the BUF was driven by opposition to 'the Reds' and hatred of 'the Jews'. Antisemitism was central to the ideology and politics of Mosley and the BUF, "all sections of the BUF were united in their hatred of the Jews".[21] For both Hitler and Mosley antisemitism was used ruthlessly. Hatred of 'the Jews' motivated their own fascist party members, but also it projected to their followers a fake explanation of the crisis ridden capitalist system of the 1930s.

The return of fascism

The events that this book focuses on took place nine decades ago in the 1930s. In 1945, the fascist regimes in Italy and Germany were destroyed. The liberation of Auschwitz and the other death camps revealed to the world the full horror of the Holocaust. Fascism, we were told, had been thrown into the dustbin of history for good. Lessons had been learned. Liberal democratic states would never again collapse like they did in the interwar years. This was always too complacent a view. In the 1970s in Britain, for example, the Nazi National Front made significant gains.

But today, no one prepared to look at reality can deny the serious threat we face. The liberal political centre is collapsing, unable to deal with the multiple crises it has ruled over: from vast social inequalities to cost of living crises, global pandemics, looming ecological catastrophe, wars and rising tensions between major powers. Mainstream parties try to shore up support through racism and authoritarianism, but the result is only to further boost the far right and fascists.

In the United States, Trumps' second term as president is even more brutal and racist than his first. Armed, masked ICE agents are unleashed on black, Asian and Latino communities, and anyone who is willing to stand in solidarity with them. Would-be Trump's elsewhere, like Brazil's Bolsonaro or South Korea's Yoon Suk Yeol, have attempted coups, just as Trump did when he encouraged a mob of his supporters, including fascists like the Proud Boys, to storm the US Capitol building on 6 January, 2021.

In Europe, Marine Le Pen took 41.5 percent in the 2022 French presidential elections. Her party, National Rally, is knocking on the door of power. And despite its claims to have "de-demonised" and moved away from its fascist past – claims simply taken at face value by mainstream politicians and media – it remains a fascist party.[22]

In Italy after elections in September 2022, one hundred years after Mussolini came to power, Giorgia Meloni and her Fratelli d'Italia ('Brothers of Italy') formed a government. The Fratelli stand in a "70-year tradition of Italian fascism".[23] Meloni is proud of the 'flame' in her Fratelli party logo which evokes her roots in the fascist Movement Social Italiano (MSI), a party founded after the war by devotees of Mussolini, which used the same image. As a fifteen year old Meloni joined the MSI which had been established by veterans of "Mussolini's Nazi-collaborationist Italian Social Republic, the Salo Republic".[24] Today Meloni is full of praise for Italy's fascist dictator Mussolini: "Everything he did, he did for Italy – and there have been no politicians like him for 50 years", she has said.

Her successful election campaign slogan echoed the language of fascist Italy: 'God, Fatherland, Family'.[25]

In Germany, Alternative for Germany (AfD) formed originally as anti-Euro party is now dominated by its fascist wing, led by Björne Höcke. The AfD came second in the 2025 German parliamentary elections. In Austria, the Freedom Party, created by former Nazi SS veterans in 1956, topped the polls in the 2024 elections. In Spain and Portugal, both ruled by dictatorships until the mid-1970s, far right and fascist parties have made huge gains.

The authoritarian regime of Viktor Orbán in Hungary is a model for much of the far right across Europe, a stepping stone towards the type of society they want to create. Orbán's election campaigns have exploited the "incessant demonisation of George Soros", a financial investor and liberal philanthropist, and "best known in his native Hungary as a rich Jew".[26] The Hungarian leader made light of the Nazi gas chambers in Second World War when he criticised an EU plan to cut gas demand by 15 percent, pointing out that "the past shows us German know-how on that". In a speech in 2022, Orbán said, "We Hungarians are willing to mix with one another, but we do not want to become peoples of mixed race".[27] Orbán claims that it was "the Jew" Soros who brought all the unwanted migrants and Muslims into Hungary. This demonisation of Muslims and migrants carries with it a turn towards antisemitism – the old antisemitic story of a 'global network of Jewish power' together with racism against Muslims who are considered to be 'terrorists'.

Islamophobia is the central public form of racism that today's fascists use to build support. But in his book *The New Age of Catastrophe*, Alex Callinicos explains why antisemitism still remains important today "especially for fascists, because of its role in continuing to provide the basis for a pseudo-critique of capitalism that locates the source of the problem not in the system, but in the corrupting effects of 'cosmopolitan Jewish finance capital'".[28] Hidden behind phrases like "globalism", the language may be more 'coded' but the antisemitic reality hasn't changed.

But the victory of such forces is not inevitable – provided we learn from the past and how to apply its lessons today. In Britain in the mid-1930s the forward march of Mosley's BUF was halted by a mass anti-fascist mobilisation – a tradition that has continued to shape the struggle against fascism in Britain.

The anti-fascist tradition in Britain

The myth that fascism is simply not British and that "foreign ideologies like fascism and Nazism will never take hold on these shores … it is just not in our character"[29] is exactly that: a myth.

Organised fascists in Britain have repeatedly been able to win considerable support and establish fascist organisation; the BUF in the 1930s, the National Front (NF) in the 1970s, the British National Party (BNP) in the 1990s and 2000s.

In the 1970s the Anti Nazi League created a mass movement that smashed the National Front.

In the 2000s the BNP, founded in 1982 by former members of the NF, saw its support grow. By 2009 the BNP had gained "a total of 940,000 votes winning two seats in the European parliament, as well as a member of the Greater London Assembly, and close to 60 local councillors".[30] A series of mobilisations led by Unite Against Fascism (UAF) beat back support for the BNP; on the Isle of Dogs in London, and then in local strongholds in Burnley, Stoke and Barking and elsewhere they were defeated and driven out of all of their council seats.[31] With support of the Northwest TUC, UAF organised a 'Nick Griffin Must Go!' to kick the BNP's leader out of his European parliamentary seat. The campaign broke the electoral support for the BNP in the northwest region. It was this sustained opposition that defeated the BNP; they splintered and collapsed.

In 2009-2010 a fascist street movement, the English Defence League, centred on Islamophobia, emerged led by Tommy Robinson (real name Stephen Yaxley-Lennon), a former BNP member. Mass mobilisations by UAF defeated the EDL which eventually collapsed.

In 2017-18, racism was at the heart of the thousands of 'Football Lads' who organised marches which were increasingly influenced by Robinson. Stand Up to Racism mobilised to oppose them. When Robinson tried to get elected in the 2019 European elections in the northwest region a mass 'Use Your Vote to Stop the Fascist Tommy Robinson' campaign succeeded in stopping him. Robinson won just two percent of the vote.

But in 2024-25, once again the racism of both the Tories and Labour, together with the rise of Nigel Farage's racist far right Reform UK, boosted the confidence of street racists and fascists. In the summer of 2024 a wave of racist riots, pogroms in all but name, took place outside hostels and hotels housing refugees. Mass mobilisations in August 2024 by Stand Up to Racism broke their momentum. But a new wave of anti-refugee protests took place in the summer and autumn of 2025.

And in September 2025, Tommy Robinson called and led an anti-refugee and Islamophobic march in central London of 100,000, maybe more – far outnumbering the anti-fascist counter protest. This was the biggest fascist-led march in British history.

But we *can* turn the tide.

In Britain anti-fascist struggles have been shaped by a political tradition of socialists applying the united front tactic to stop fascist parties and movements growing. From the Battle of Cable Street in 1930s, to opposition to the NF and the BNP, the historical record shows that effective opposition to fascism in Britain has been organised, not by mainstream political parties, but by the forces on the left, by working class militants.

We live today in an era where established political leaders are increasingly discredited, pedalling racism instead of solutions to the acute economic and political crisis, environmental catastrophe, and war. These are the conditions in which fascist forces are growing. The anti-fascist struggles that halted the advance of Mosley and the BUF in the 1930s won mass support in working class communities. These are struggles that can inform and inspire us today in the fight we face against racism and fascism.

This book sets out to show that the events at Cable Street were not isolated or a one off, but were the culmination of a *national* anti-fascist movement, especially in the years 1934 and 1936 when the BUF pushed hard to breakthrough. The book also pays particular attention to a group of young Communists, many of the Jewish, in Manchester who played a central role in combatting the BUF.

Mark Krantz
January 2026

Chapter 1 describes the growth of fascist forces across Europe in the 1920s and 1930s – Mussolini and Hitler, as well as Oswald Mosley and his party of antisemitic Blackshirts, the BUF.[32] Mosley and the BUF hated 'the Jews'.

Chapter 2 explains Jewish migration and the development of antisemitism. Opposition to Mosley in Manchester was spearheaded by a group of young communists who met in Cheetham Hill and called themselves the Challenge Club.

Their struggles and the lives of some of the leading anti-fascist activists are described in **Chapter 3**.

Communist politics from the Russian Revolution, the setting up of the Comintern, Stalin's disastrous policies, and the eventual adoption of a united front to oppose fascism in Britain are explained in **Chapter 4**.

The organised anti-fascist resistance in 1934 when Mosley spoke at BUF rallies in small towns and big cities across the country is described in **Chapter 5**.

Chapter 6 shows how, in 1936, across Britain local anti-fascist committees were able to mobilise even greater numbers in direct confrontation with Mosley and the BUF, leading up to the Battle of Cable Street in London's East End.

The 'united front' policy of opposition to fascism led by communist party[33] members was short-lived; replaced by the 'Popular Front' policy. **Chapter 7** explains this shift, and how it impacted on the struggles against fascism in France, Spain and Britain.

Chapter 8 charts anti-fascism after Cable Street.

Chapter 1
Fascist forces grow across Europe

Mussolini and the Blackshirts in Italy, 1919-22

Two 'red years' of mass struggles and strikes in Italy terrified the bosses and landowners. The *Biennio Rosso* years began in the summer of 1919 when Italian workers launched a two-day general strike. At the end of August 1920 militancy reached a climax when, following a demand for higher wages, engineering workers in Milan were locked out by their employers. Workers responded by occupying their factories: "From the great urban areas to the country districts… wherever there is a factory, a dockyard, a steelworks, a forge, or a foundry in which 'metalos' worked, there was an occupation."[34] The occupation of factories marked the high point of a wave of workers' struggle in Italy. But the occupation of the factories ended in a confusing compromise, not a revolutionary struggle for power.

"While the left debated the failure of the occupation of the factories, industrialists and large landowners moved into action."[35] They offered their support to Mussolini and his party, the 'Fasci Italiani di Combattimento'. The month after its foundation in March 1919, the first act of fascist violence occurred as Mussolini's men organised a physical attack on left wing demonstrators in Milan. This was followed by an armed attack on the offices of *Avanti!*, the Socialist Party daily newspaper. "This type of *squadrista* 'action' – an assault on a building, followed by looting, violence, burning and destruction – was to be repeated thousands of times over the next few years."[36]

Mussolini's fascist squads physically attacked and destroyed militant organisations of workers and peasants. They broke up picket lines, beat up trade union militants and poor peasants' leaders. They burnt down socialist meeting halls and trade union offices and killed elected officials. His squads of fascists wore distinctive blackshirt uniforms. The police stood by or joined in these assaults. Fascist squads and police attacks killed thousands of working-class people.[37]

Italian big business leaders, fearful there would be a revolution in Italy as had happened in Russia in 1917, offered Mussolini financial and political support. In 1922 Mussolini organised his fascists to 'March on Rome'. They were escorted through the streets by the army and then marched back out. Mussolini's fascist movement did not come to power through winning elections or simply through a violent overthrow; Mussolini was appointed prime minister by the King of Italy, Victor Emmanuel III. Under Mussolini Italy was transformed into a totalitarian regime with 'Il Duce' as the all-powerful fascist leader.

The "Roman genius" impressed Winston Churchill

In 1927, five years after the fascists took power in Italy, the British chancellor of the exchequer Winston Churchill went to meet Mussolini in Rome. Churchill "was convinced early on that Mussolini and Italian fascism represented the only kind of extra-parliamentary force capable of defeating the Russian communists and their followers in Europe. The fascists could mobilise people in the streets, something that traditional conservative parties could not".[38] Churchill later referred to Mussolini as the "Roman genius", proclaiming "your movement has rendered a service to the whole world".[39] Churchill was clear:

If I had been an Italian I am sure I would have been whole-heartedly with you from the start to finish in your triumphant struggle against bestial appetites and passions of Leninism. But in England we have not yet had to face this danger in the same deadly form.[40]

Adolf Hitler takes power in Nazi Germany, January 1933

When acute economic collapse hit the German economy in the early 1930s Hitler and his Nazi Party started to gain significant support. Mass unemployment caused economic devastation. The middle classes abandoned their traditional parties, many turning to Hitler. Hitler had an answer. His message was that the communists and the Jews were the cause of all the economic strife in Germany. Central to Hitler's political ideology was antisemitism. On 30 January 1933, the German President Paul von Hindenburg appointed Hitler as Chancellor of Germany. Shortly after, in late February, the German Reichstag parliament building was burnt down in a fire. This was used as an excuse to ban the German Communist Party, who the Nazis blamed for the attack. Mass repression began. The historian Donny Gluckstein explains why this was allowed to happen:

Most workers saw through the Nazi lies and voted socialist or communist. Millions belonged to unions. Despite unemployment every factory, railway, and power plant depended on workers to function. But this force was never used because the left was fatally divided.[41]

The socialists and the communists opposed each other; they failed to unite. Hitler faced no organised, united resistance. On 22 March the first concentration camp opened at Dachau near Munich. The next day stormtroopers intimidated the remaining German parliamentary deputies into supporting an Enabling Act which gave Hitler the power to introduce any measure he wanted without democratic approval. A new period of terror opened. Now Germany, as well as Italy, were run by fascist dictators.

Life in the early 1930s

Those alive in Britain in the 1930s had grown up in a period of acute economic crisis combined with political turmoil. Turbulence and uncertainty, challenge and betrayal characterised the period following the First World War. In 1919 industrial militancy, strikes and demonstrations brought Britain almost to revolution, but the trade union leaders were unprepared and unwilling to take power.[42] The 1926 General Strike in Britain went down to defeat, called off by the trade union leaders at the TUC General Council after just nine days, when it was gaining momentum.[43] These defeats demoralised the workers' movement.

In 1929 the Wall Street Crash in New York triggered a worldwide financial crisis. The Great Depression that followed brought severe economic strife, unemployment and hunger. Austerity brought suffering to the working class. The middle class worried for their savings and lost the economic certainty they once enjoyed. The 1929 general election saw a Labour government take office. Bankers and financiers demanded the new government bring in cuts to welfare spending to 'balance the books'. By 1931, these demands for massive cuts and more austerity led to a split in the Labour cabinet as the party leader Ramsay MacDonald and others left to join with the Tories to form a National Government.[44] The Tory-led National Government brought in a further cut of 10 percent to unemployment benefits, the wages of teachers, civil servants, the police and those in the armed forces. The response was a series of demonstrations,[45] riots,[46] and hunger marches.[47] A naval mutiny broke out.[48] In this period of economic distress, with the political betrayal from a Labour government that crumbled and split, and more austerity brought in by the National government, the would-be fascist leader Mosley set up his fascist party in Britain.

After Italy and Germany, will Britain be next?

Sir Oswald Mosley was born into an aristocratic family. In the 17th century Sir Nicholas Mosley had enclosed land at Collyhurst, near Manchester. The "principal residents of the town resisted the attempt" but were unsuccessful and the Mosley family, through force and deception, acquired the land on which Manchester stands.[49] With the development of Manchester as an industrial city, the Mosley family invested, expanding their wealth and power even more. Streets in the city centre carry the family name: Mosley Street and Lower Mosley Street. From birth Oswald Mosley, as a hereditary peer, became the Sixth Baronet of Ancoats. After officer training at Sandhurst military college, he joined the war in 1914, was injured and discharged. He then went straight into politics and at 21 years old he was selected for the safe Conservative seat of Harrow.

Later, rejecting the politics of the Tory Party, he left and went on to join the Labour Party, where he was welcomed. Mosley won a by-election in Smethwick for Labour and became a "promising junior minister in the Labour government of 1929" where he "put forward a bold plan to combat the depression of the early 1930s by making the empire a closed economic zone, and spending, into deficit if need be, for job creating public works and consumer credit".[50] This "scheme of national economic planning"[51] won approval from the economist John Maynard Keynes. The leaders of the Labour Party were wedded to free market 'laissez-faire' economic policy. They rebuffed these proposals. Mosley resigned and formed his own New Party in 1931. After complete failure at the ballot box, Mosley began looking for a new political strategy. He found it after a visit to Mussolini in Italy – fascism.

It was meeting the fascist leader 'Il Duce' (the leader) in Rome that "persuaded the frustrated Mosley that fascism" was a movement of the future that "would be his own personal way forwards".[52] He was accompanied by Captain Lewis, who would become the first editor of the BUF's paper *Blackshirt*, along with "a contingent of 12 uniformed British fascists".[53] Mosley took part in the fascist 'Birth of Rome' festival, and "held private conversations with Il Duce on the subject of international fascism in general and his own work in Britain". Mussolini agreed to fund Mosley's party; regular secret cash donations of £5,000 were organised.[54] On his return to London Mosley told the *Daily Mail* that it had been a great experience: "It is, I believe, a step towards universal fascism."[55]

Blackshirt Mosley gains support

Mosley modelled his party, the BUF, on Mussolini's party, complete with blackshirt uniforms. When Mosley formed the BUF in late 1932 he promised 'ACTION!'. The main slogan was 'Britain First!'[56] Mosley promised that "fascism alone will deal faithfully, with the alien menace, in whatever quarters it rears its head".[57] The BUF newspaper *Blackshirt* was launched in February 1933. In the first issue Mosley declared, "It is important to demonstrate the BUF's ability to stand up to Communist disorder".[58] In his *Ten Points of Fascism* programme Mosley made political promises in which:

The workers were promised work; the middle classes were promised protection from the Bolshevik workers; the capitalists were promised better and more stable profits; the trade unionists were promised freedom from capitalist exploitation; the landlords were promised economic security; the small farmers were promised more land and guaranteed prices; the aristocratic families… were promised a proper respect for their traditional status; the nation was promised deliverance from decadent feudalism.[59]

His appeal struck a chord; "New members poured into the BUF at a rate never equaled by any other political party or movement". It was small tradesmen, shopkeepers, ex-army and ex-navy officers, and small professional people, who swelled the ranks of the BUF. While the bulk of the party was middle class there were some workers who joined Mosley's party. Active in the BUF were former Labour Party and Independent Labour Party (ILP) members John Beckett, Charles Dolan and Robert Forgan. "By the beginning of 1934 the number of active BUF branches in the country was 400, with 50 members to each branch."[60]

Within the eight months from October 1933 to June 1934 the BUF staged great meetings at the largest halls in Manchester, Liverpool, Birmingham, Oxford, Sheffield, Edinburgh, Derby, Portsmouth, and Newhaven. The practice was to transport great contingents of Blackshirts – mostly the toughs of the Fascist Defence Force – from one centre to another to create the impression of great strength. As many as two to three thousand Blackshirts were often mustered for such occasions. The cost of transporting and of feeding these armies was born by the BUF central funds, which were estimated to be in the region of £70,000.[61]

The toughs of the Fascist Defence Force were the most loyal, hardline members of the BUF, paid and deployed by Mosley. The Fascist Defence Force acted as the organised militia of the BUF. Mosley claimed in his book, *Fascism in Britain*, that "the purpose of the Fascist Defence Force is, in fact, entirely defensive. It is organised to protect our meetings and propaganda from the organised violence of the reds".[62]

Mosley and the BUF won the support of some of Britain's most powerful newspaper barons, big industrialists, as well as members of the royal family. The Prince of Wales, in line to become King Edward VIII, was a keen supporter. He had "fascist leanings and sympathy with the Nazi cause and the corporate state in Italy". He was "proud of his German origins, spoke German fluently, and felt an emotional, racial and intellectual solidarity with the Nazi leaders". The prince "was quite pro-Hitler and said it was no business of ours to interfere in Germany's internal affairs either re Jews or anything else, and added that the dictators are very popular these days, and that we might want one in England before long".[63]

Several major capitalist corporations – Imperial Chemical Industries (ICI), Courtaulds Textiles and the car manufacturer William Morris – gave money to Mosley's party. The millionaire publisher Lord Rothermere, who owned the *Daily Mail* and many regional newspapers, was one of Mosley's key political backers. The *Daily Mail* ran a front page with the headline 'Hurrah for the Blackshirts!'. On 15 January 1934 an editorial by Rothermere declared that Britain needed a "well organised party of the right ready to take over responsibility for national affairs with the same directness of purpose and energy of method as Hitler and Mussolini have displayed".[64]

Antisemitic Blackshirts

While Mosley modelled his fascist organisation on Mussolini's Blackshirts, he followed Hitler in using antisemitism to both provide motivation for his BUF activists, and to use 'the Jews' as a scapegoat for popular discontent. From its foundation, antisemitism was at the heart of Mosley's BUF party. "At the very first public event, at London's Memorial Hall in October 1932, Mosley's address contained two key components of antisemitism".[65] This involved hatred against Jews because they were foreign, and labelling Jews as traitors to Britain. According to Mosley, Jews had an alien and dangerous culture and identity, they held great power and wealth, and their presence damaged the economic interests of the British people.

Inside the Mosley meeting there was opposition from a noisy group in the audience who Mosley acknowledged and condemned as "class warriors from Jerusalem".[66] He dismissed his opponents, denigrating them for being class conscious workers who were Jewish. From 1933 onwards the number of articles in the BUF newspapers that mentioned Jews in a negative context steadily increased.[67] Mosley said in September 1934 at his Belle Vue rally in Manchester that "Jews, more than any single factor are undermining the prosperity of the British people today", and he "could not tolerate those who sabotage the nation".[68] This was the rabid antisemitism of the BUF.

Chapter 2
Jewish immigration and antisemitism

Who were the Jews that Mosley despised?

The Sephardic, or Spanish, Jews were the first to settle in Manchester. They had escaped the repression in Spain in the 15th century. Living in the south of the city, most prospered working in the professions, in banking, as jewelers, or in trade. By the end of the 19th century the majority of Jews in the world had fled repression in Europe and moved eastwards. Millions lived in what was the Russian empire. These were Ashkenazi Jews; 'from the east'. They were forced to live only in restricted areas in the Pale of Settlement.[69]

Under the dictatorial and repressive regime of the Russian Tsars religious repression against the Jews increased. In the late 19th century, there were protests against the Tsarist regime. Workers, peasants, and students demanded change; they wanted justice, reform and democracy. The Tsar responded with brutal repression and racism. He encouraged attacks on Jews, using antisemitism to 'divide and rule'. In the 1880s a series of pogroms against Jews took place. In the early 1900s, a paramilitary group, the Black Hundreds, was unleashed. Their battle cry was 'Kill the Jews and Save Russia!'. They massacred hundreds of Jews.

Many fled for their lives. For the Jewish refugees the favoured destination was the United States, however many made it only to England, most settling in the East End of London, but also in Manchester and Leeds. Some settled in Scotland. The Ashkenazi Jews who made Manchester their new home lived in the north of the city around the district of Cheetham Hill. They worked in small factories and workshops, spoke Yiddish and learned English.[70] Dozens of synagogues were built, a rich cultural and religious community developed.

There was, however, a class divide within the Jewish community. A small minority of Jews were rich manufacturers and mill owners. Most Jews, though, worked in the small factories and workshops, making raincoats, umbrellas and clothing. From their homelands in Russia and Poland these working-class Jews brought with them experience of building trade unions and socialist organisations, which had flourished in Russia. Many had belonged to the Jewish socialist trade union organisation, the Bund.[71] Others followed revolutionary or anarchist traditions.[72]

On arrival the Jewish immigrants set up their own trade unions. The Manchester Jewish Machinists, Tailors and Pressers Trade Union was created in November 1888, "to fight for better pay and conditions". In 1889 with support from Manchester and Salford Trades Council "the union launched its first successful strike".[73] That was "a year of massive class struggles" in which many Jewish trade unions were set up: "By 1896 there were 13 Jewish trade unions and double that number by 1902."[74] Jewish trades unionism was an effective response to the antisemitic jibe that the "Jewish aliens, in accepting low pay and savage working conditions, were undercutting the livelihood and well-being of the native workforce".[75]

The British government wanted to keep Jews, especially poor Jews with radical political traditions, out of the country. In 1905 to stop more coming into Britain they brought in a special Act of Parliament. Racist from its inception, the Aliens Act was the country's first immigration law. The Manchester Tory MP Arthur Balfour had long called for the introduction of immigration controls.[76] Arguing for the Bill in parliament, Balfour said:

Are we to be bound to support every man, woman, and child incapable of supporting themselves who choose to come to our shores? That argument seems to me to be preposterous. When it is remembered that some of these persons are a most undesirable element in the population and are not likely to produce healthy children... but they are afflicted with disease either of mind or of body, which makes them intrinsically undesirable citizens, surely the fact that they are likely to become a public charge is a double reason for keeping them out of the country.[77]

The Aliens Act kept out those without "the means of decently supporting himself and his dependents". The poor Jewish undesirable immigrants were stopped from entering Britain. A more hostile environment for Jews followed the 1905 Aliens Act. In 1924 Britain's Tory Home Secretary William Joynson-Hicks publicly deprecated "those who put their Jewish faith before their English nationality". He said he feared "an England flooded with the whole of the alien refuse from every country in the world". *The Times* newspaper agreed, describing immigrant Jews as an "alien element in our land". In the 1930s Britain's rulers were openly antisemitic.

Manchester's Jewish workers in the 1930s

The Jewish population in Manchester faced many changes and challenges in the 1930s as "the economic structure of the Jewish Quarter, created by the immigrants of the late 19th century, was gradually ceasing to provide a secure and comfortable livelihood for their children". The "workshops were closed without notice, hours were shortened and pay cut in many that remained open. Less scrupulous masters replaced skilled union labour with cheap labour, unskilled workers, many underpaid on the pretense of them being 'apprentices'".[78]

Aubery Lewis lived in the Cheetham district of Manchester: "My childhood was spent in acute economic difficulty. I was born in a working-class district at a time of economic recession. I was eleven years old when the Wall Street Crash happened. I remember vividly the effects and so many people in the area out of work, people literally dropping from starvation. People tried to commit suicide in the area where I lived."[79] It was this "dismal economic climate in Lancashire as a whole in the early 1930s that persuaded Mosley to make Manchester an important focus of his blackshirted BUF".[80]

A fascist headquarters in the heart of the Jewish community

Two lines of uniformed Blackshirts gave the fascist salute for Oswald Mosley as he opened his northern headquarters. Each wore a uniform comprising a "black shirt and trousers and a broad leather belt, every single Blackshirt was equipped with a little black truncheon hanging from his hip pocket".[81] The BUF now had an operational fascist headquarters in the centre of Manchester's working-class Jewish community. From this base Mosley's thugs went about terrorising people; they marched around the streets chanting "The Yids! The Yids! We're gonna get rid of the Yids!".

Maurice Levine was a young Jewish worker living in Cheetham Hill. He recalled how in 1934:

The BUF had its headquarters in Northumberland Street in Higher Broughton. A favourite café of theirs was Walter's on Great Ducie Street near Victoria Station, and they would walk through the Strangeways district, along Bury New Road to Northumberland Street to provoke the Jewish population – there would often be scuffles with the inhabitants of Strangeways.[82]

At their Northumberland Street headquarters, the BUF had one full-time northern regional organiser, as well as nine other staff. From here they organised the BUF in the region, setting up branches across Greater Manchester and the surrounding Lancashire towns. The BUF soon had branches in Miles Platting, Stretford and Altrincham as well as Bolton, Bury, Blackpool, Rochdale, Accrington and Preston. The BUF had 5,000 members in Lancashire alone. By the end of 1934 there were also BUF branches in Ashton-under-Lyne, Hulme, Rusholme, Withington, Blackley, Salford, Oldham, Southport and Fylde.

With the once mighty textile industry in the northwest in decline, when Mosley spoke in the Lancashire region, he claimed it was the Jews who were financing the Indian cotton industry, thus devastating production. He promised that a fascist government would exclude Japanese cotton products from Empire markets and shut down competing Indian mills. Mosley promised he would also deal with the Jewish capitalists who invested in foreign markets.

The official response to the rise of the BUF

The leaders of the trade unions and the Labour Party, elected councillors and MPs, the chief rabbi and Jewish leaders of the Board of Deputies of British Jews together shaped the official response to Mosley and the antisemitism of the BUF.[83] They all agreed that it was best to ignore him. They told their members not to protest against the fascists.

The leadership of the Labour Party blamed the communists for the rise of fascism; they equated communists with fascists. Labour issued a special statement entitled *Democracy and Dictatorship* which alleged that "Communist dictatorship or fear of it had led to fascist dictatorship".[84] The lie told by the Nazis that German Communists had burnt down the German parliament building was not challenged. For the Labour leaders the communists were considered a bigger danger than the fascists. Fascism would be beaten by argument and education alone. The leader of the Labour Party, Clement Attlee, debated Mosley at the Cambridge Union, giving respectability and publicity to the claim made by Mosley that "only fascism could secure order out of the economic chaos which exists today".[85]

Labour leaders would debate with Mosley, but never share a platform or debate with CP members. The leader of London City Council, Herbert Morrison, advised that "Jews should keep in the background" and not confront the fascists.[86] The Labour MP Fielding West said of those anti-fascists who shouted down Mosley at a rally at London's Olympia: "We in the Labour Party do not fear the effect of Mosley's speeches. In any event let him be heard."[87] Leslie Lever, a Jewish Manchester Labour councillor who would become an MP and Lord Mayor of the City, "opposed a proposal to bar the leasing of public halls to fascists, on the grounds that while Jews had every reason to abhor fascism, they, of all people, should understand the importance of protecting basic rights such as free speech".[88] When it came to how to respond to Mosley's fascists, the Labour and trade union leaders' position was clear and consistent: Never confront the fascists, stay away from them and their meetings, and protect free speech for all – including the race hate speech of Mosley and the BUF.

Jewish community leaders speak out

Neville Laski was born in December 1890 and grew up in Manchester. He became a leading figure in the local Jewish community and went on to become the leader of the Board of Deputies. As a young child Neville's father, Nathan, had emigrated from Russian Poland. His mother was from Lithuania.

In Manchester Nathan Laski had set up a business and became a rich cotton merchant. He had his son educated at Manchester Grammar School, Clifton College, and Corpus Christi College, Oxford. Neville Laski practiced as a barrister in Manchester and became a Queen's Counsel. In 1930 he moved down to London to become the President of the Board of Deputies.

Laski was now one of the most prominent leaders of the Jewish establishment in the country. On 12 May 1933 he appealed to Jews to avoid violent activity and opposition to the BUF which "can only be harmful to the general cause which we all have at heart". Appearing "impeccable and blameless to the outside world was the best answer we could give fascism", he said.[89]

The Board of Deputies consistently maintained this approach, "imploring Jews not to involve themselves with militant antifascism".[90] The Chief Rabbi Joseph Hertz agreed. He too cautioned against anti-fascist action, warning that Jews' wellbeing "largely depended on the morality" of their own behaviour.[91] The editor of the *Jewish Chronicle*,[92] Jack Rich, in response to reports of noisy protests against Mosley, condemned the "stupid and disgraceful behaviour of the Jews involved, who by copying Nazi violence which we loath and detest, were betraying the Jewish cause". The paper followed up with an interview with Mosley who used it as a platform to claim that "charges of antisemitism were a lie designed to discredit his party", the BUF.[93]

The Manchester School of Zionism

As well as being the home to many Jewish anti-fascists in the 1930s, Manchester was the home of the leading of political Zionist, Chaim Weizmann. Zionism was a political ideology that developed as a response to antisemitism.[94] For Zionists non-Jews are considered as 'naturally' antisemitic and the only solution to antisemitism is for Jews to separate themselves from non-Jews.

When, in 1904, Weizmann arrived as an émigré he took up a post at the University of Manchester as a lecturer. He described the political environment in Manchester as: "…frightful, in fact beyond description. You are dealing with the dregs of Russian Jewry, a dull ignorant crowd that knows nothing of issues such as Zionism."[95] Weizmann was disparaging about the lack of support for Zionism from the working class Jews in Cheetham Hill.

Working with some middle class Jews, Weizmann was successful in building "a local network of Zionist activists and supporters which became known widely as the 'Manchester School of Zionism'".[96] Amongst them was Harry Sacher, a journalist on the *Manchester Guardian*, his friend from Oxford, Leon Simon, Simon Marks[97] and Israel Sieff.[98] The group would meet at Sieff's home in Didsbury in South Manchester where their ideas would be debated. They wrote for the *The Zionist Banner*.[99] At the World Zionist Conference[100] Weizmann won a political argument that a future "homeland for the Jewish people should be – not in Russia, Uganda or Brazil, but in 'Palestine'".[101]

As a chemist studying at Manchester University, Weizmann developed materials used to make bombs for the British army. His bacterial fermentation process allowed large-scale, domestic acetone production. This meant faster and cheaper manufacturing processes that were a major boost to British munitions capacity during the First World War.[102] Weizmann gave the bomb making copyright to the British. This aided Weizmann in his discussions with Arthur Balfour. On 2 November 1917 the "British Government, represented by Arthur Balfour, declared the establishment in Palestine of a national home for the Jewish people".[103]

Throughout 1934, as BUF fascists were attacking Jews on the streets, Weizmann and the Zionist group played no part in the resistance to the antisemitic attacks from the Blackshirts.

One young Zionist publication declared that Mosley's racism against the Jews created an 'opportunity' to garner support for Zionism. One headline proclaimed: "The Hitler Menace: Will its Effects Prove Beneficial to Jewry?"[104] Further "the German Jews suffering should be treated as a lesson – with the fascists as the 'most cruel of teachers'" – that the only way forwards was "a united Jewry with its own country" in Palestine which would act as a "bulwark" against antisemitic attacks.[105] To seek "'proactive alliances' with gentiles, would be a sign of 'Jewish weakness'".[106] "The Zionist leadership's primary concern was not the growth of British fascism itself, but the fact that it was pushing Jews into the arms of the Communist Party."[107] Rose Henriques, the well-heeled founder of a prominent Jewish girls club in the East End, wrote with concern to the parents of her young charges that "a great many … have joined the Communist clubs, not because they are Communist but because they feel that the Communists were the only people who were trying to fight the Fascists".[108]

Abuse from the thugs in the BUF

Advice to ignore the fascists was of little help when Mosley's thugs shouted racist abuse as they marched down the streets where Jewish people lived, held race hate meetings in the local park, and shouted "the only paper not owned by Jews" as they sold the *Blackshirt* outside cinemas and dancehalls. With Mosley's thugs terrorising Jews in working class communities, many young Jews physically defended themselves. Maurice Levine explained:

> At a personal level one to one fights would very often break out following antisemitic abuse. A verbal encounter would often lead to physical attacks. Many of my contemporaries would not stand for it. It would end up in fisticuffs on the

spot, maybe on a bus, maybe in a cinema queue, maybe in a dance hall. Any reference to 'Jew boys' could end in a fight. That was common as anything. My immediate reaction to any expression of fascism was; knock their bloody head off![109]

In contrast, Jewish community leaders continued to oppose all confrontation. Laski only once attended a BUF street meeting "to see what it was like". He was shocked and offended. In public he continued to call for restraint, but in private correspondence to the Tory home secretary, the President of the Board of Deputies admitted; "Any self-respecting Jew in the crowd would have the greatest difficulty restraining himself, not only vocally, but physically" when exposed to antisemitic abuse from the thugs in the BUF.[110] Laski was able to choose to go and see for himself the racism of the BUF. For poor Jews like Levine it was impossible to avoid such abuse, personal self defence was a necessity. But individual action was not enough to stop the BUF thugs, a collective response was needed.

Chapter 3
Building mass opposition to Mosley and the BUF: the Manchester example

The Cheetham Hill branch of the YCL was central to the resistance to Mosley, antisemitism and the BUF in Manchester. Who built the Challenge Club?[111]

The Ainley brothers

Solomon Abrahamson was a Lithuanian Jewish immigrant. He arrived in Manchester in the 1880s. Solomon was a skilled artisan working in local factories making walking sticks and umbrellas. His wife, who had just arrived from Latvia, ran a tiny tobacco and newsagent shop on Great Ancoats Street in the heart of the Irish and Italian working-class district. In Lithuania Solomon had been a member of the Bund. As a socialist now living in Manchester, he named his first-born son Maurice, after the English socialist William Morris. Now with a new life in England, Solomon changed his surname from Abrahamson to the anglicised Ainley. Three of his other sons, Ben, David and Teddy were central to setting up the YCL branch in Cheetham Hill:

> Ben was one of a group of secularised Jews, all children of Jewish immigrants from Eastern Europe, and most of them like Ben, unemployed, who in 1919 began to meet informally at the Ainley home to debate political issues. Calling themselves the 'Pioneers', they were in fact, in the vanguard of young Jews,

born and brought up in Manchester, who had begun to reflect critically upon the social and economic circumstances that were defining the prospects of immigrant Jewish families... by 1921 'the Pioneers' had begun to consider the Communist option.[112]

During 1922-23, Ben, David and Teddy became the founder members of the YCL branch set up by the Communist Party in Cheetham Hill. Other members of the Pioneers who also joined the YCL branch were: Gabriel Cohen, Joe Cohen, Hymie Lee and Johnny Rosenbloom.[113] Ted Ainley joined the Communist Party in 1923. He became a party organiser, leading demonstrations of unemployed workers. In 1933 he set up a *Books and Books* bookshop on Great Ducie Street. Ted Ainley helped develop a network of local correspondents for the *Daily Worker*, the Communist Party's daily paper. By 1934 Ted Ainley, along with Jack Flanagan and Jim Cunnick, had become one of the triumvirate which was responsible for leading the CP in Manchester.[114]

Benny Rothman: from the Kinder Scout Trespass to anti-fascism

Benjamin (Benny) Rothman was a keen walker. He helped establish the British Workers' Sports Federation (BWSF) and soon became its secretary for the North, organising rambles, camping and cycling weekends in the Peak District. While out walking with friends in the hills on their Easter ramble in 1932, bailiffs who were there to keep the open land in private hands stopped them, blocking their way. "We were humiliated by the bailiffs", said Rothman, when he reported back to the other walkers at their base camp in Derbyshire. They talked through what had happened and decided to make a call for others to join them in a month's time for a 'mass trespass'.

Hundreds of mainly young men and women came from Manchester and Sheffield to join the Kinder Scout protest.

They defied the bailiffs and walked onto what was in law private estates used to raise grouse for aristocrats to shoot for sport. The bailiffs and the police cracked down on the protesters. Amongst those arrested was Benny Rothman. He had just turned twenty-one and was up on charges of riotous assembly, assault, and incitement at Derby Assizes. At his trial Rothman read out a prepared statement:

> We ramblers after a hard week's work, and life in smokey towns and cities go out rambling on weekends for relaxation, for a breath of fresh air and for a little sunshine. And we find when we go out that the finest rambling country is closed to us. Because certain individuals wish to shoot for about ten days per annum, we are forced to walk on muddy crowded paths, and denied the pleasure of enjoying to the utmost the countryside. Our request for access to all peaks and uncultivated moorland is not unreasonable.[115]

He was jailed for four months. Four other young people in the dock with him were also imprisoned from two to six months. After serving time in prison Rothman joined the Challenge Club in Cheetham Hill. He became a leading anti-fascist:

> We had a very strong YCL branch in Cheetham with nearly 200 members, I was branch secretary for a while. We had bags of energy and enthusiasm and we were determined to beat the Blackshirts. We felt that it was something we had to do, not only because we were Jewish, but also because we were communists. We found a way of working with other anti-fascists who might not agree with the Communist Party on other

issues. We had a room above a garage in Hightown, which we used for film shows, political discussions and sporting activities. We held regular Sunday dances, which were very well attended and used it as a base for rambles and cycle rides. It became the main focus of our lives for a number of years.[116]

Evelyn Taylor

Evelyn Taylor was one of hundreds who joined the mass trespass at Kinder Scout and she too was active in the YCL. Taylor joined the National Council of Labour Colleges and worked in a number of engineering factories in Manchester. When she was fired from her job at Ferguson & Pailin's factory for her union activity she appealed to the National Society of Brass and Metal Mechanics to organise a strike; the workers came out, she won reinstatement. As an 18-year-old in 1931 Taylor joined the CP.

At Mosley's first public meeting in Manchester, Taylor heckled him and later helped disrupt his BUF rally at the Free Trades Hall. Mosley took out a private prosecution against her for leading anti-fascist protests that had curtailed his free speech. She was found guilty and fined £25. In court Taylor told the magistrate she had "not come to hear Mosley speak and was determined that no one else should". She refused to pay the fine and appealed her conviction. The appeal was rejected by the Recorder of Manchester, Sir Walter Greaves-Lord, who concluded:

I think people are a little apt to think that under the idea of free speech there exists a free and unlimited right of interruption, which, carried to its complete conclusion, would make free speech quite impossible and would destroy one of the very greatest liberties we possess.[117]

Evelyn still refused to pay the fine. She was sent to Strangeways prison.

Maurice Levine

"We seemed to be involved in anti-fascist activity on an almost daily basis. If we weren't organising our own meetings, we were trying to stop the fascists from holding theirs", said Maurice Levine, describing life in the YCL. In 1934 there was a big strike at Richard Johnson & Nephew in Openshaw over a 'time and motion' plan.[118] Strikebreakers were brought in from outside, and the CP organiser suspected they were members of the BUF. "I was asked to go to the factory, wait around until the shift finished and follow the men to see where they were living. I did this getting on the tramcar with them and they finished up at the Northumberland Street premises that was a barracks for the Mosley fascists in Manchester."[119] Mosley's men were involved in organised scabbing on strikes, as well as racist attacks against Jews.

Bernard McKenna

Bernard McKenna was born in 1915 to Irish-English parents living in the working-class Hulme area of Manchester. He was the seventh child, but extreme poverty meant his six elder siblings all died in infancy. At 14 he became a textile mill clerk working in a clothing factory in Cheetham Hill, owned by one of the area's Jewish businessmen. "I joined the Labour League of Youth in 1932 when I was 17, but left to join the YCL two years later. I was much happier in the YCL because there was a more socialist feeling about them." Later, as a member of the CP "I took part in protests against all the Blackshirt meetings and joined in attempts to disrupt them".[120]

Jewish anti-fascists like Rothman and Levine joined non-Jewish gentiles like Taylor and McKenna to lead the fight against the BUF – gentiles and Jews united in the fight against the fascists.

Chapter 4
Communists, the Russian Revolution and the United Front

It was action against the fascists that drew young people like Benny, Evelyn, Maurice, Bernard and many more to join the CP in Manchester. The Manchester branch was vibrant. CP members had led unemployed marches, supported strikes, and fought for access to the countryside.

The CP was one of a number of similar parties that had been set up across Europe in the aftermath of the 1917 revolution in Russia.

What happened in the Russian Revolution?[121]

Protests started by women over shortages of bread in February 1917 led to demonstrations, strikes, and then mass protests. Striking workers and revolutionaries set up workers' councils, called 'soviets' in Russian. The Tsar Nicholas II was overthrown, and the democratic rule of elected soviets replaced the dictatorial rule of royal, Tsarist ministers. In March a revolutionary provisional government led by capitalist ministers was established, promising to bring Russia out of the war and provide help for the impoverished, but these leaders failed to deliver any of the changes people had fought for.

In August a virulent antisemite, the Russian general Kornilov, armed and financed by western powers, led an army to march on and destroy the revolution. His plan was to kill all the revolutionaries and murder the Jews. It was Leon Trotsky who led the defence of the revolution.[122] Trotsky built a movement that united all those who agreed that the revolutionary government must be defended, and Kornilov must be stopped. A united front of resistance halted the counter-revolutionary general in his tracks: "Had he won, the word for fascism would not have been an Italian, but a Russian word".[123]

By October the revolutionary Bolshevik party, now led by Lenin and Trotsky, gained mass support from workers and poorer peasants with these central demands: All Power to the Soviets! Bread, Peace, and Land! The Bolsheviks led a second revolution in October, and a new communist state based on the rule of workers' councils was established. The Bolshevik Party became the Communist Party. Along with their supporters internationally the communists now set about trying to spread revolution to other countries, to build a worldwide movement, and to defend the gains made by the revolution in Russia:

> The Communist International, which arose out of the Russian Revolution of October 1917, was not an optional extra but essential, indispensable part of that revolution, which in turn, was part of an international revolutionary upheaval.[124]

The Comintern

The Bolsheviks formed the Communist International, known as the Comintern, in 1919. It was set up to bring together the best militants from across the world to form parties that could repeat the Russian victory. Delegates from labour and socialist parties met in March 1919 and thereafter at a series of Comintern conferences at which policies and resolutions were agreed to help advance proletarian revolution internationally.[125] The Russian leader Lenin argued that it was essential that revolution be spread to other countries. Lenin believed that what was needed most was a successful revolution in Germany. A revolutionary movement did erupt, "Germany from 1917-1923 was the scene of the greatest working-class revolutionary upsurge ever in an advanced capitalist country".[126] Chris Harman explained its significance – and the impact of its defeat:

> Here was a great revolutionary upheaval, in an advanced industrial society, and in Western Europe. Without an understanding of its defeat, the great barbarisms that swept Europe in the 1930s cannot be understood – for the swastika first entered modern history on the uniforms of the German counter-revolutionary troops of 1918-23, and because of the defeat in Germany, Russia fell into the isolation that gave Stalin his road to power.[127]

By 1923, after a long struggle, the German revolutionary movement ended in defeat. The despair arising from the victory of counter-revolution helped fuel the growth of Hitler and his Nazi Party.

The defeat in Germany meant that the new communist state in Russia was now even more isolated, the resources to build socialism further weakened. Out of these conditions, and after a brutal internal and bloody struggle against those who had led and defended the revolution, a new leader in Russia took over, Joseph Stalin. Stalin abandoned the project of advancing world revolution. Instead, he advocated "socialism in one country". The politics of Stalinism "was not simply a response to isolation" of the Russian state, "it also perpetuated that isolation".[128] Under Stalin's leadership the early revolutionary perspective of the Comintern was replaced.

By 1928 this involved a new 'sectarian' period in which the Communist parties cut themselves off from the wide layers of workers who were influenced by trade union and social democratic organisations with the claim that revolution was now on the immediate agenda.

Stalin developed the policy of calling for 'revolutionary advance' soon after the workers movement suffered two major defeats; the General Strike in Britain (1926)[129] and the revolution in China (1925-1927).[130] Despite these defeats Stalin in 1928 told Communists in every country that "they were now in a new 'third period' of revolutionary advance".[131] Nevertheless Stalin was able to strengthen his rule over both the Russian party and the Comintern. Pushing the 'adventurous' third period policy Stalin was able to blunt criticism from within the Russian party that his policies in Britain and China had failed because they were too cautious. And at a time when the Russian masses faced acute deprivation arising from forced industrialisation,[132] Stalin used support for the third period policy as a mechanism to "weed out anyone in the international movement who might conceivably criticise what was happening" to people in Russia. It also led to "the imposition of policies on Communist parties in the rest of the world which damaged the chances of revolution".[133]

It was during the 'third period' that Stalin oversaw "the final transformation of foreign Communist parties into organs of Russian foreign policy".[134] The American revolutionary James P. Cannon described the consequences of Stalin's bloody counter-revolution. He said that Stalin had turned the communists from being "agencies of revolution into border guards of the Soviet Union and pressure groups in the service of its foreign policy".[135] The Comintern now became "more and more dominated by considerations, not of international socialist revolution, but of Russian foreign policy" decided by Stalin.[136]

In Germany the outcome of these policies proved catastrophic. The German Social Democratic Party (SPD) was an established mass left wing political party supported by the trade unions. The SPD secured millions of workers' votes in elections.[137] Stalin argued that the biggest danger facing the Communist parties was the social democratic leaders and their members. He slandered them all as 'social fascists'. The social democratic parties like the SPD in Germany and the Labour Party in Britain were treated as if they were a greater threat than the fascist parties.

Stalin sent these instructions to the British CP in 1928: "In our general campaign against the Labour Party we should emphasise that it is a crime equivalent to blacklegging for any worker to belong to the Labour Party."[138] Being a Labour Party member was considered equivalent to being a strike breaking scab. Communist trade union militants were expected to refuse to work with or alongside militant workers aligned to the Labour Party. In 1929 at a meeting of the Comintern, "Stalin's representatives gave final formulation to the doctrine of 'social fascism' according to which fascism was in the process of being introduced in countries like Germany and Britain by their respective social democratic parties".[139] When the CP General Secretary Albert Inkpin raised criticism of the party's line of not working with others on the left he was replaced, with Stalin's approval, by Harry Pollitt. The new General Secretary was a reliable advocate of the CP 'party line' of opposing the policy of a united front against fascism. Under Pollitt's leadership the CP championed the view that the Labour Party was a greater threat to the working class than the fascist Mosley.

The Left Opposition calls for a united front against fascism

After the 1929 economic crash that devastated German economy, support for Hitler in Germany grew sharply. With mass unemployment and an established political class with no answers or solutions, Hitler gained a hearing. In the final round of the presidential elections in April 1932, Hitler polled over 13 million votes. By June the Nazis, protected by police, had started street battles in working-class suburbs. There were heroic fights by communists against the Nazis, but no united opposition to Hitler.[140]

A small group of CP members in the Balham branch in south London were alarmed and concerned at developments in Germany, alongside the increasing isolation of CP members in Britain. These comrades would become the Balham Group, part of the British Section of the Left Opposition.[141] They published and distributed some of Trotsky's writings in a duplicated journal, including *Germany: the Key to the International Situation* where Trotsky warned that support for Hitler in Germany was growing and that fascism was a serious danger for the working class.

To discuss this the Balham Group organised a series of open-air meetings. Reg Groves explained the reason: "We showed solidarity with comrades in Germany and we hoped that the German CP might be persuaded to make an eleventh hour offer of an organisational united front with the social democrats (the German SPD) against the Nazis." At one meeting in July 300 people met on Clapham Common to hear a broad platform of speakers from the labour movement: "two trades union leaders from engineering and transport sectors, W. Jordan from the Labour Party, three speakers from the ILP, along with Saklatvala, Stewart Purkis, and Reg Groves from the CP".[142] The CP member Shapurji Saklatvala had been the local MP from nearby Battersea, twice elected to parliament. Known widely, he was a "hugely popular figure among his white working class supporters".[143]

The national leadership of the CP sharply criticised the meeting organisers as it was not the agreed party line. Reg Groves and other members in the Balham Group were suspended from the party, then expelled, and the Balham CP branch was closed down. At a special meeting of London CP members Reg Groves and his comrades were denounced and derided for wanting "a united front with the vile social democrats!".[144] While the communists and the socialists were focused on their political differences in Germany, the Nazis organised the destruction of democratic institutions and working class organisations. They seized on the burning down of the German parliament to blame the Communists. On 27 February 1933,

> The German Reichstag was set on fire, a dire combustion that in due course was to burn much, much more than the German parliament. Immediately, the German CP was made illegal, Nazi terror unleashed, thousands of social democrats and communist officials and members arrested. Consumed in flames too was the disastrous policy imposed by Stalin's men on the German party and the Comintern.[145]

The Comintern opens the door to a united front policy 1933-1935

Hitler's stormtroopers, facing no united and organised opposition, completely destroyed the German Communist Party. At the time, it was the largest Communist Party in the world with millions of members and supporters. Following this victory for Hitler the political line of Stalin and the Comintern changed.

A new political line was developed. Communists should work with the very people they had previously denounced as strike breaking blacklegs. In their book the *History of Communism in Britain* the writers Brian Pearce and Michael Woodhouse explain how, "between the beginning of 1933 and the middle of 1936 the International communist movement underwent one of the most startling transformations of policy in all its history".[146] From Moscow the new line for the Communist Parties was to advocate a united front against the fascist threat, and to call for unity with other political trends. "The campaign for a united front only commenced in real earnest when Hitler came to power in March 1933."[147]

Only in Britain was there any "substantial progress in actually achieving a united front".[148] There was little guidance on how the CP should apply the principle. Initially the CP's leadership focus was on relations with the ILP.[149] As Pearce notes "voices were heard saying that the Communist Party was doing the right thing (belatedly) for the wrong reasons". But a space for CP members on the ground to seek to work with wider forces in the working class against Mosley and the BUF movement now existed: "It was the CP rank and file, not the leadership, which campaigned."The *Daily Worker* recorded many local initiatives.[150] As Mosley set about building his fascist party in Britain, those out to oppose him were encouraged by this new CP line. Armed with a 'united front' policy CP members became the central force directing the fight against the BUF, antisemitism, and Oswald Mosley.

Chapter 5
1934: the fightback against Mosley begins

It took years of struggle and mass protests to hold back and defeat Mosley and his fascist thugs. Mosley toured the country in 1934 and again in 1936 speaking at rallies and meetings, establishing local BUF branches. The BUF mobilised nationally, with plenty of funds for coaches and trains.

Anti-fascists organised locally, building mass opposition to Mosley when he rallied or marched in their town or neighbourhood. The first anti-fascist protesters were individuals who asked Mosley questions, then a few heckled him. They were met with extreme violence from the BUF stewards. In response anti-fascists protests grew in size and determination to stop Mosley's fascist party. Local activists had an international outlook, they read the news reports of the fascist victories in Europe, the growth of the rising fascist powers in Italy, Germany, Austria, and Spain. With Mosley on the doorstep at home and fascism spreading across the continent, tens of thousands of working-class people responded by joining mass anti-fascist protests against the BUF. The history of their struggles is told here.

On New Year's Day 1934, the *Manchester Guardian* reported on Nazi terror.[151] One of their reporters had just returned from the Dachau concentration camp in Germany. He described the organisation, routine and recent history of the camp, considered by the German Nazis who ran it as a 'model' camp. The practice of isolating enemies from the larger civilian population and 'concentrating' them outside of the familiar framework of jails and prisons was not invented by the Nazis,[152] but they "perfected the concentration camp" and Dachau established a standard for the massive SS-run network of camps:[153]

> A prisoner sentenced to detention in one of the cells gets nothing to eat on the first day, then bread and water for three days, and a hot meal every fourth day. The number of prisoners is 2,200-2,400. Of these about fifty are intellectuals, a few are members of the middle class, without any political affiliations, fifty or sixty are Nazis, about sixty are Jews, about five hundred are Socialists, two are army officers, there are several beggars and ordinary criminals, fifteen are non-German subjects, and the remainder are Communists. The overwhelming majority belong to the working class. The student Wickelmeier was killed by a bullet. The Communist Fritz Dressel was beaten to death. Leonhard Hausmann, a municipal councillor, Lehrburger, Aron and Stenzel were all killed.[154]

As reports of the horrors of the German Nazis and their concentration camps became public knowledge, Mosley was organising fascist rallies across Britain where support for – as well as opposition to – fascism grew. The anti-fascist movement successfully held Mosley and the BUF back through mass protests. The movement was made up of "members of the CP, the Labour Party, the Quakers, the Catholic church, trade unionists, community groups and many other political, social and cultural organisations"[155] as well as members of the ILP.[156] A sign of the mass anti-fascist protests to come in 1934 took place in Teesside in the autumn of 1933.

The Battle of Stockton, September 1933

By early 1933, "the BUF had established a small nucleus of an organisation on Teesside, centred on Stockton… Small towns and semi-rural areas hit hard by unemployment were seen as prime areas for recruitment for Mosley's fascism. Minus the strong opposing political culture of the big industrial cities which partnered a local well-organised trade union and labour movement, they were seen as easy pickings for the BUF".[157] The initial attempts by the BUF to hold street meetings in the town, "met determined opposition from members of National Unemployed Workers Movement (NUWM), the Independent Labour Party (ILP), the Labour Party and Teesside Communist Party". The BUF responded by planning a rally in Stockton on 10 September 1933.[158] But news of the rally got out, and anti-fascists mobilised:

> On the morning of that day, fully loaded motor coaches carrying… over 100 BUF members from Tyneside and the Manchester area, set off for Teesside… the disembarked blackshirted and jack-booted phalanx of Mosley's army to begin their march along Stockton High Street. They were not alone, however. An opposing crowd, according to contemporary press accounts, some 2,000 strong, was ready and waiting in ambush. The BUF managed to get as far as the Town Hall building in the middle of the High Street market place but any further progress was halted by the sheer weight of numbers of their opponents.[159]

Anti-fascists proceeded to storm the stage the BUF had set up. The local police were caught off guard and were overwhelmed. They ordered the BUF to halt the meeting and leave the town: "Scurrying down the High Street, a group broke off to attack the counter demonstrators. [But] encircled, they fled … and found themselves effectively kettled in Silver Street, a narrow lane linking the High Street to what was then Stockton's working quayside. Here, the fighting really got going and the first BUF casualties recorded, with twenty more to follow." Eventually, the Blackshirts had to run the "gauntlet" of anti-fascists to get back to their coaches.[160]

Mosley heckled at his first meeting at the Kings Hall, Manchester, October 1933

When Mosley announced he would be speaking at a meeting in Manchester, anti-fascist groups in the city got together and debated what to do about it. In the end it was decided to not directly oppose Mosley but hold a rival public meeting in the Free Trade Hall on the same night.[161] Rothman had "reservations on the wisdom of this and was determined to go to the Mosley meeting under his own steam". He described what happened at the BUF meeting at the Kings Hall:

Inside the hall there was a tense hysterical atmosphere. Then came a rolling of drums and a blare of trumpets, and preceded by a small army of strong arm stewards, and followed by another group of stewards with the drum and the trumpet, accompaniment rising to a crescendo. Mosley bounded into the hall and onto the platform to a spotlight mounted with microphones and of course decorated with a huge Union Jack. Sections of his supporters stood up and became hysterical in their clapping and cheering as Mosley, resplendent in his tailor-made black uniform, melodramatically raised his arm to call for silence.

Gradually silence was restored and Mosley started to

speak in a dramatic voice and manner. He had hardly started when an interruption came from a spot in the balcony opposite me. It was a woman's voice which I recognised right away as belonging to Evelyn Taylor. She stood up and started to shout and heckle.[162]

Mosley signalled and women Blackshirt stewards were sent in to silence her. The BUF Woman's Section were trained in jujitsu.[163] She fought them off. Male stewards were sent in. Appalled and angered by her beating, Rothman, who was in the balcony, threw a pile of anti-fascist leaflets into the air. Blackshirt stewards attacked him, with shouts of "come here you yiddisher bastard".[164] They threw him over the balcony, his fall broken by a Blackshirt below.

Mosley had been heckled at his first public meeting in Manchester. He was outraged. Mosley would later complain about what happened, how his free speech had been interrupted. Outside the Kings Hall, Rothman joined a small group who had been thrown out of the fascist meeting:

> Unlike me most of them had fared far worse than I had, and one or two had sustained a bad beating. We had a short discussion and decided to go to the Free Trade Hall where one of the group made a short statement on what had gone on in Kings Hall. Some lessons could be learned from these events. It was clear that if the opposition had really wanted they could have closed Mosley's rally.[165]

From then on, direct confrontation and disruption of Mosley's meetings replaced the tactic of holding separate protest meetings in another part of town whenever he spoke.

Mass rally at Manchester Free Trades Hall, March 1934

On 12 March, at Manchester's largest venue, the Free Trades Hall, Oswald Mosley spoke to 4,000 people with the protection of 130 BUF stewards. Hecklers were persistent. The BUF stewards were brutal. Prior to the meeting Manchester fascists had for weeks been Jew-baiting prominent Jews who they shadowed and subjected to all sorts of insults. BUF activists painted walls with the death threat 'Perish the Jews'. There was an attack on three Jews by a group of Blackshirts outside the meeting hall.[166]

After his speech Mosley took questions. Someone in the audience asked Mosley: Is your organisation antisemitic? Before the question was answered a Blackshirt drew his truncheon and hit the man from behind. He crumpled up. As people in their seats rose in confusion the Blackshirts hit out blindly with their truncheons in all directions. Witnesses spoke of a man with "blood streaming down his face, being battered by a gang of a dozen Blackshirts".[167] When other members of the audience stood up to object they too were assaulted. Fighting spilled over into the aisles. So great was the violence that the Manchester police went into the meeting to eject the BUF stewards. The *Manchester Guardian* reported that "a small man who had been fighting with the fascists gave the police a rubber hose on a string saying he had taken it from a steward".

When later Mosley was challenged in the press about BUF stewards wielding rubber hoses as truncheons, he announced that in future BUF stewards would be banned from carrying such weapons. Two days later, anti-fascists protesting against a BUF meeting outside Rochdale Town Hall were attacked by Blackshirts armed with knuckle dusters and lead filled rubber hoses.[168] After the fascist violence at his Free Trades Hall meeting the local authorities refused Mosley permission to book the hall again, nor would he be able to secure any venue in central Manchester.

Community support for the YCL

Though the YCL's membership was not large, it could count on widespread sympathy for its anti-fascist activity, with a "whole community involvement" from Jews and non-Jews in working class areas.[169] The YCL had an effective and well-oiled system of mobilisation which sprang into action the moment their spies in the BUF informed the YCL leadership of Blackshirt plans. Aubrey Lewis recalled:

> The moment news came, say of a fascist march or street meeting, there was a network immediately. It was a close-knit area: terraced houses, streets close by one another, everybody on foot, people used to legging it. You used to get on a bike, race round the area and our first weapon to mobilise was a leaflet. We used to run off leaflets like a flash. Printers in the area were sympathetic to us. Someone would knock on the door one evening. Come out with us we've got leaflets to give out.[170]

Manchester was just one of a number of towns where militant anti-fascist resistance to the BUF was organised. Throughout 1934 there were militant anti-fascist protests against Mosley's BUF across the country. Action against Mosley was not limited to members of the CP. Members of the Labour Party and trade unions took part in spite of their leaders' strident opposition to confrontation as a method of opposing fascism. Protests also took place in towns where there were few, if any, Jewish people living.

Newcastle and Gateshead, May 1934

On 13 May a crowd of several thousand anti-fascists stopped BUF organiser Beckett from speaking at an outdoor rally in Newcastle upon Tyne, rushing the platform he occupied at Cowen's monument. Earlier, some thirty fascists had left the BUF headquarters on Clayton Street en route to the Beckett meeting. "There were scuffles, then uproar due to an attack on a Communist worker in Blackett Street, rolling into another fight on Westgate Road… several of the Blackshirts pursued their opponents into doorways, knocked them down, and were in turn struck down." Where the Blackshirts' rally was scheduled to take place "an enormous crowd of thousands refused to give Mr Beckett a hearing and called him a traitor".[171]

Beckett recalled in his memoirs how, when he got up to speak, "a thousand anti-fascists rushed the platform and pandemonium broke loose". Police told the BUF to abandon their meeting. Mounted police escorted them – with their injured – back to their headquarters. But the anti-fascists did not go away. They laid siege to the fascist offices placing it under a heavy rain of missiles. According to Beckett "every window was broken in the large branch room with its floor covered with blood and groaning men, it was a gruesome site".[172] After the anti-fascists had dispersed, many went on to a rally at the Haymarket where the ILP Glasgow MP James Maxton spoke, calling for a united front against fascism. The following day an even greater number mobilised in neighbouring Gateshead to prevent Beckett speaking at a BUF rally there. A reporter for the *News Chronicle* described what happened:

> The police had to clear a path for Beckett's escape; crowds of more than ten thousand people were driven back and sixty fascists were escorted to their headquarters by mounted cycle

patrols. As the Blackshirts got halfway across the Tyne Bridge a section of the crowd attempted to rush the party, seemingly intent on throwing the fascists in the river.[173]

Edinburgh and Glasgow, June 1934

In Edinburgh Mosley faced protests when he rallied hundreds of uniformed Blackshirts, many of them bussed in from the north of England, who clashed with anti-fascist opponents after the close of BUF meetings. Glasgow was home to around 15,000 Jews, the majority living in areas of the Southside such as the Gorbals and Govanhill, where they opened synagogues, youth groups and shops. Mosley faced opposition when he came to speak here. The *Glasgow Herald* reported in June 1934 that several thousand anti-fascists trapped fascists in their headquarters and that only police intervention got them out.

Monty Berkeley, a Communist Party member, shared his own memories of how he and his comrades took to the streets to face the Blackshirts head on when BUF speaker Joyce came to Queen's Park recreation ground: "We organised a counter demonstration with a number of us from the working class, the Labour League of Youth, Young Communist League and other youth organisations all agreed to disrupt the meeting. I had the privilege of taking one of the platform legs and throwing the platform up in the air."[174]

London Olympia, June 1934

In June the BUF organised a showcase rally at London's Olympia arena. Ahead of their rally 'Perish Judea' was painted by fascists on walls, calling for Jews to be killed. Fifteen thousand came to hear Mosley speak. Over 10,000 anti-fascists protested, some inside, but most outside the hall.

The fascist rally was intended to impress the ticket holders with the "political divinity of its leader, the virility of his pro-gramme, and the efficiency of his Blackshirt followers in action against their political opponents"[175]. London's Fascist Defence Force turned out in full strength, well briefed and trained for the task of the evening: "Its number swelled to thousands by contingents from as far as Liverpool. Many of them wore kid gloves, concealing knuckle dusters or heavy rings."[176] They took up positions in groups of half a dozen or so at all points in the Olympia amphitheater. On the slightest interruption a signal would be flashed for them to go in.

When a man in the audience asked Mosley, "Does Hitler stand for free speech?" he was immediately set upon and attacked. One Tory MP present described how he was "appalled by the violence of the fascists". Widespread press coverage and many eyewitness reports exposed the shocking violence of the BUF stewards. Mrs. Naomi Mitchison had gone to Olympia with three friends to see Mosley speak. She too was appalled by the violent attacks. In her eyewitness report she explained how she was revolted by those in the neighbouring gallery who were "Mosleyite sympathisers, some of them wearing the fascist badge. After each interruption they began to show more and more excitement. They cheered with increasing enthusiastic pleasure" at the beatings being dealt out to hecklers.[177] A Tory MP in the audience told the *Yorkshire Post* how he witnessed people being "attacked by ten to twenty fascists. Again and again, as five or six fascists carried out an inter-rupter by arms and legs, several other Blackshirts were engaged in hitting and kicking his helpless body".[178]

While many were revolted by the violence of Mosley's thugs, his supporters were impressed by the brutality of the Fascist Defence Force whose actions were described in the German press as "marvellous". The Nazi controlled newspapers acclaimed the "energetic defence of the Blackshirts in a bloody battle".[179]

Mosley in Wales, July 1934

Just a few hundred Jews lived in Wales in two small communities in Cardiff and Swansea. In April 1934 Mosley went to Cardiff with Tommy Moran, ex-light heavyweight champion of the Royal Navy and a former miner who had joined the BUF. Mosley wanted Moran "to connect with the miners".

When Mosley was denied a booking for a rally at the large Cory Hall in Cardiff, he complained that this was due to Jewish influence.

When in July Mosley returned to Wales for a rally at the Plaza Cinema in Swansea, 10,000 anti-fascists turned out to oppose him. It was the miners' unions and the local CP that organised the opposition to Mosley in Wales. As usual after his speech Mosley took questions from the audience; "I work for a Jew. Should I change my employer?" Mosley replied, "I am disgusted that anyone should work for a Jew. You should be certain to find a more reliable gentile". Up stood the questioner to reveal his dog collar. The Rev Leon Atkins' 'employer' was Jesus Christ! The huge audience erupted attacking the Blackshirts. Mosley was rushed away shouting "Blasphemy! Blasphemy!" Amongst the anti-fascist protesters that day was the 19-year-old Dylan Thomas. "I was there and was thrown down the stairs", said the future poet and author.[180]

Hyde Park, London, September 1934

Anti-fascists mobilised in London's Hyde Park on 9 September to oppose another Mosley rally. A statement from the official Labour Party, Trade Unions, Co-Ops and The National Council for Labour, signed by Walter Citrine, the TUC general secretary, and Arthur Henderson, a former leader of the Labour Party, called on workers to have nothing to do with opposing Mosley's rally in Hyde Park.[181] The CP roundly condemned this statement.

They produced an *Anti-Fascist Special* which sold thousands. Pollitt wrote in the *Daily Worker*, "you cannot argue with a tiger" and that Mosley and the BUF must be opposed by mass protests, not argument and discussion. "Detailed planning of the march to Hyde Park was very comprehensive and was published on the back page of the *Daily Worker*".[182] Preparations were "undertaken by the Co-Ordinating Committee for Ant-Fascist Activity".[183] One million leaflets were printed to publicise the protest.[184] The Communist Party issued a special leaflet in Yiddish.[185] During one organ recital broadcast live on the BBC, activists grabbed the microphone and managed to say "March against fascism; All to Hyde Park on 9th September" before being switched off.[186] Despite the TUC calling for all trade unionists not to attend, many trade unionists were among the 150,000 anti-fascists who surrounded and swamped the 2,500 BUF fascists who were cordoned in by 6,000 police.

"Drowned in a sea of working-class activity" was the headline in the *Daily Worker* report of the day:

> The huge protest was built by throwing leaflets from the roofs in Whitehall, hanging banners from the BBC HQ and from the Law Courts, and chalking on pavements. The Communist Party united with ad-hoc groups, and trade union and Labour Party left wingers to form the Committee for Anti-Fascist Activities, they called the counter-demonstration to confront the fascists.[187]

The *Manchester Guardian* commented the next day: "If this counter demonstration, which outnumbered Mosley's by twenty to one, could be gathered from such a small party as the Communists, with large numbers of Londoners acting on their own initiatives, on what scale would the opposition have been had it had the whole force of Labour behind it?"[188]

Manchester march against Mosley at Belle Vue, September 1934

After the huge protest at Hyde Park, anti-fascists building in Manchester for the next protest at Belle Vue on 29 September published a leaflet with the strapline: 'Follow the Lead of the London Workers!'[189] Printed in Manchester, this leaflet was distributed by anti-fascists outside factories and in localities across the city. Five thousand people opposed Mosley at his BUF rally in Belle Vue Gardens. Unable to secure a Manchester hall for his showpiece rally, Mosley had booked a venue outside the city centre in east Manchester. The Belle Vue complex with halls, gardens and a lake was a popular entertainment venue for workers. When in mid-September word got out of his plan, the newly formed Manchester Anti Fascist Campaign started distributing leaflets outside factory gates urging that "Belle Vue be turned into a workers' stronghold".[190]

Three days before the rally the Manchester and Salford Trades Union Council met. After a three-hour discussion a motion was agreed that the Trades Council would not support the protest demonstration against Mosley's Blackshirt rally.[191] Instead it was resolved that they would organise an anti-fascist conference – at some time in the future.[192] The next day the police declared the anti-fascist march unlawful. Thousands of names had been collected on a petition, drawn up by CP member Maurice Levine, demanding that Mosley should not be allowed to hold his fascist rally at Belle Vue. In a letter sent with the petition to John Maxwell, the Chief Constable of Manchester, Levine called on him to either ban the BUF rally or allow a counter march to take place.[193] Maxwell's response to the petition was to issue a proclamation: a curfew would be imposed and all marches would be banned. As it was only the anti-fascists who were building for a march, it was only the anti-fascist action that had been declared unlawful. Mosley's rally, with police protection, could go ahead.

Mosley charted a special train to bring 500 fascists from London, and coaches were hired from across the region to bring hundreds of fascist supporters to Manchester to see and hear their leader Mosley at a showcase rally.[194] He faced mass opposition. Lack of official union support, opposition from the local politicians, and an outright ban from the police did not stop those determined to confront Mosley from marching against him. Anti-fascists had been preparing for weeks, going all out to build the march to oppose Mosley and stop him on the day.

"We did a great deal of work, calling on people to come out to stop the Mosley rally", recalled McKenna. "We handed out leaflets, held street corner meetings and chalked pavements and walls all over the place. There were three separate anti-fascist marches on the day. Each one set off from a different part of the city and we all met at Ardwick Green."[195] On the day the police made no attempt to stop them. The *Manchester Guardian* reported:

The biggest march was from Cheetham Hill and comprised in the main young working-class Jewish activists from the Challenge Club, the YCL formed the backbone of the group. Among banners and emblems carried was the red flag, but also the St George's flag. A group from the Anglo-Catholic movement joined the march. Contingents of the Youth Front Against War and Fascism from Leeds and from Sheffield were there, as was a contingent from the Bolton branch of the NUWM, and the Manchester anti-war council. A group of women marched with their own banner; Women Unite Against Fascism![196]

When the marchers arrived at Belle Vue, they were greeted by hundreds of protesters who had already assembled. After a short rally they went into the Belle Vue complex. Journalists from the *Manchester Guardian* described what happened:

Once we were inside we saw a microphone and amplifiers set up on the gallery and that the area in front had been sealed off with wooden barricades. Behind the barricades were hundreds of police. Not a single Blackshirt could be seen. Suddenly, five hundred Blackshirts marched out of the halls in military formation. Mosley, aping Mussolini, stepped forward to the microphone to speak. As soon as Sir Oswald appeared on the platform the presence of a compact and rowdy opposition force declared itself. The Blackshirts raised their hands to greet Mosley and cheered. From outside the barrier came boos and catcalls. For about a minute Sir Oswald stood waiting for silence. Then his voice was heard through the loudspeakers above the shouting of the crowd. An opening phrase: 'The assembly of this great crowd on a wet evening…' was partially audible to one standing on the fringes of the assembly, but after that an organised chorus of shouting drowned the speaker's voice completely. Mosley was greeted by a wall of sound that completely drowned his speech.

Down with fascism!
Down with the Blackshirts!
The rats! The rats! Clear out the rats!
One, two, three, four, five! We want Mosley dead or alive![197]

"Anti-fascist songs, the Red Flag, and the Internationale were sung. The sound never stopped for over an hour. In spite of the powerful amplifiers turned up to maximum Mosley could not be heard."[198] The *Manchester Guardian* reporter said, "Sitting in the midst of Sir Oswald's personal body-guard within three yards of where he was speaking one was barely able to catch two consecutive sentences".

Militant, organised, anti-fascist resistance had stopped Mosley from being heard by his fascist supporters.[199] As Mosley's rally was ending, recalls McKenna, "The only sound they could now hear was the singing of 'Bye! Bye! Blackshirt!'", an anti-fascist adaptation of the popular song of the time, *Bye Bye Blackbird*.[200] The anti-fascists were singing while the BUF hid their colours as they made their way back to their coaches and the special train back to London.

Plymouth, Devon, October 1934

Active fascists lived in every corner of Devon. The BUF regional headquarters was in the naval town of Plymouth, "home to more than a thousand fascists". Mosley made many visits to the area, and "BUF branches were formed throughout the county and many thousands of local people were drawn to meetings".[201] On 16 April, the BUF held a meeting at the Corn Exchange, with Beckett as the main speaker. It was disrupted by anti-fascist protesters. When he left the meeting "the waiting crowd of both sexes tried to attack the fascists as they carried the Union Flag and marched to Lockyer Street" with a police escort. Opposition to the BUF was spearheaded by CP members, around "thirty communists were actively agitating" against BUF, their opposition "strengthened by other organisations including Friends of Soviet Russia, International Labour Defence, and the NUWM".[202]

On 5 October Mosley returned for a mass gathering, this time at the Drill Hall. Mosley flew by private plane from London to Plymouth. He went on to speak at a rally to a crowd of "between 3,500 and 4,000 people". He had 50 BUF stewards at the meeting. A large group of protesters interrupted Mosley's speech by singing the *Red Flag*. As the Fascist Defence Force stewards tried to silence the protesters, Mosley turned up the loud speakers; it fused the electricity in the building and the already tense room was thrown in to darkness. The Blackshirt stewards hit out randomly, and a photographer from the local paper was badly injured, his camera smashed. Police entered the building 'to restore order'. When Mosley left "several thousand anti-fascists, waited outside".[203] After the Drill Hall rally the local press blamed his stewards for the violence and BUF stewards faced police charges for violently assaulting the photographer. The tide of political support turned against Mosley in the county.

Worthing, the 'Munich of the South', October 1934

The BUF held a string of meetings in early 1934 in the seaside towns of Worthing, Chichester, Bognor and Rustington, along the West Sussex coast. They held annual fascist summer camps at nearby Pagham, Selsey, and West Wittering.[204] The weekly *Fascist News* described the growth in BUF membership in Worthing as "phenomenal" after 150 people joined at one meeting in January. The mayor of Worthing, Harry Duffield, leader of the Conservative Party in the town, "was impressed with the Blackshirts and congratulated them on the disciplined way they marched through the streets of Worthing".[205] Employers in the town, he said, had written to him "giving their support for the British Union of Fascists". Worthing bosses had "no objection to their own employees wearing the blackshirt even at work".[206]

Worthing had the first fascist councillor in Britain. Charles Bentinck Budd had been elected as an independent with "well known fascist views" who, after meeting Mosley, joined the BUF. Worthing was described as the "Munich of the South".[207] When Mosley came to speak here, he was expecting a warm welcome. When he spoke at a BUF rally at the Pavilion it was packed with hundreds of cheering fascist supporters. Mosley told the crowd how he had recently been "assaulted by the vilest mob you ever saw in the streets of London – little East End Jews, straight from Poland".[208] He said that "Britain's enemies would have to be deported. Are you really going to blame us for throwing them out?"[209]

After the BUF rally, uniformed fascists emerged with Mosley from the Pavilion: "There were 2,000 angry people waiting outside. The crowd surged forward and several fights began. When the Blackshirts retreated inside, the crowd began to chant: 'Poor old Mosley's got the wind up!'"[210]

Chris Hare, the author of *Historic Worthing*, described what happened next:

Mosley left the Pavilion and, protected by a large body of Blackshirts, crossed over the road to Barnes's cafe in the Arcade. Stones and rotten vegetables were soon crashing through the windows of the cafe. Boys were observed firing peashooters at the beleaguered fascists, while some youths were taking aim with air rifles. Meanwhile a group of young men climbed onto the roof of the Arcade and dislodged a large piece of masonry, which plummeted to earth through the arcade, landing only feet away from the fascist leader. Things were getting too hot for the fascists, who made a run for it, their intention was to reach their headquarters, a 'fascist pub', but they were ambushed by 400 local youths.[211]

After facing mass opposition "the fascists never again tried to march en masse through the town of Worthing".[212]

Anti-fascism in Gillingham, Kent, October 1934

A single synagogue in Rochester served the small congregation of forty Jewish families who lived in small towns across the Medway district in Kent. When on 30 October Mosley arrived to speak at the Pavillion in Gillingham over 3,000 people assembled to oppose him. "On Mosley's arrival over 30 police linked arms to hold the crowd back and allow him into hall". Inside from a platform draped with the Union Jack Mosley addressed an audience of over 1,000 people, with twenty Blackshirts in full uniform guarding the hall.

At the meeting Mosley said that the BUF fought the Jews "'because they have opposed the interests of fascism and the interests of Britain". He argued that they would "have to choose whether they put Britain first or Jewry first". "While the crowd waited for Mosley to emerge from the meeting Blackshirts guarding the hall were pelted with eggs, the *Red Flag* was sung, and the chant went up 'One, two, three, four, five; We want Mosley, dead or alive!'" On Mosley's re-appearance "he was spat upon and missiles were thrown, including bottles".[213]

Chapter 6
Halting the fascist momentum

Militant anti-fascist protests against Mosley were organised across the country throughout 1934. These protests dented support for Mosley's BUF. The growing fascist momentum was broken. By the end of the year membership of the BUF had declined from a height of 40,000 down to 5,000 members.[214] Some of the BUF branches revived in the summer of 1935, as the BUF's "antisemitism reached a new virulence".[215] The BUF pushed "negative stereotypes of poor immigrant Jews with a whole range of 'rich Jew' antisemitism, intellectual racism and the vulgar conspiracy theories about Jewish plans for world domination".[216]

Nearly half of the BUF membership were concentrated in the East End of London, organised into four branches in Bethnal Green, Stepney, Shoreditch, and Hackney. The Mosleyite John Warburton explained how support for Mosley from some poor working-class families was built upon a feeling of despair. People had nothing. "The one thing they had was patriotism, and to them Mosley brought hope."[217] Within six months eighty BUF meetings were held in Bethnal Green alone.[218] The sixteen year old Stepney Labour League of Youth activist, William J. Fishman, witnessed the "fascist incursions mounted against Jews". These "attacks were stepped up as blackshirt gangs made daily, more often nocturnal, forays" into the East End.[219]

In October 1935 Mussolini invaded Abyssinia (present day Ethiopia), then an independent African country ruled by Haile Selassie. Abyssinia had been one of the few states to survive 'the scramble for Africa' by the major European powers in the late 19th century, having defeated Italy at the battle of Adwa in 1896. Mussolini dreamed of taking revenge for this defeat, aiming to carve out a 'New Roman Empire' in East Africa.[220] The Italian fascist forces invaded and conducted a massacre of over 20,000 people. The head of a Red Cross hospital reported that "this isn't a war – it isn't even slaughter. It's torture of tens of thousands of defenceless men women and children with bombs and poison gas".[221] Mosley and the BUF defended the killings, and smeared Haile Selassie as "Jewry's new idol".[222] Mosley described Abyssinia as "a barbarous Negro state" made up of a "black and barbarous conglomeration of tribes imbued with not a single Christian principle".[223] The BUF launched a mass campaign to support the invasion, and to stop the British government's imposing economic and military sanctions against Italy for their invasion of Abyssinia, a fellow member of the League of Nations.[224]

When the newsreels about Abyssinia were shown in cinemas many people in Britain reacted in horror. When "photographs of Mussolini and his two sons" were shown there was "a storm of booing and hissing unknown hitherto in these places of entertainment". But "for the emperor of Abyssinia, who looks pathetically small, there is always a burst of cheering".[225] In contrast there was widespread support for the Italian invasion from reactionaries. Rothermere's *Daily Mail* argued that if Britain opposed war on "one of the last and most backward of independent nation states, we should be hindering the progress of civilisation". Support for the war on Abyssinia led to an increase in BUF membership, which tripled to 15,000.[226]

Trotsky was clear, however, when he declared that "if Mussolini triumphs, it means the reinforcement of fascism, the strengthening of imperialism, and the discouragement of the colonial peoples in Africa and elsewhere". Trotsky's stand did not imply any political agreement with the Abyssinian regime. "When Italy attacked Ethiopia", he explained, "I was fully on the side of the latter, despite the Ethiopian [King] for whom I have no sympathy. What mattered was to oppose imperialism's seizure of this new territory".[227] The invasion and occupation of Abyssinian by Italian forces demonstrated the rising power of Mussolini's fascist state.

Despite the organisational revival of the BUF by the end of 1935, at the general election in November Mosley decided that the BUF was not prepared enough to stand candidates. He declared that he would "campaign for voter abstention with the slogan 'Fascism Next Time'".[228]

Local anti-fascist committees

In early January 1936 Mosley "addressed staff and affirmed his admiration for Nazism and a desire to emulate its methods".[229] Now, as a more open supporter of Hitler, Mosley spoke in a series of showcase style rallies. In 1934, out of the protests against Mosley and the BUF, activists had established local anti-fascist committees. In many localities "communists, socialists, trade unionists and Liberals" united and formed local anti-fascist organisations. "Parallel with the rise of Mosley's fascism" there developed "a vigorous united front of anti-fascist elements".[230] By working with others, small groups of CP members were able to mobilise thousands of working-class people into confrontations with the BUF.

The Manchester Anti Fascist Campaign was initiated by the Cheetham YCL members "to bring together wider forces" to oppose Mosley's showcase Belle Vue rally.[231] In the Northeast a patchwork of anti-fascist groupings was built in the winter of 1934, "with the NUWM, the CP as well as ILP members" all involved.[232] In Newcastle hundreds joined the Anti-Fascist League which was set up to provide a local Socialist Defence Corp capable of providing "uniformed protection for speakers at Socialist meetings". Organisers stated that the League was "open to all grades of socialists" who were sworn to "prevent Jewish pogroms".[233] The group also pledged they would "encourage and give hospitality to refugees from fascism", although strict immigration laws meant refugees from fascism in Europe were prevented from entering Britain. The Sheffield United Action Committee was "composed of representatives of several trade unions, the ILP, some co-operative organisations, the Anti-War Committee, and the CP, with 109 delegates representing 63 organisations".[234] Together they mobilised thousands to protest against Mosley in Sheffield.

In Kent, a local Anti-Fascist Campaign Committee was set up in May 1934 with the support of prominent members of Chatham Labour Party, including the local Labour parliamentary candidate (and future Labour leader) Hugh Gaitskell, the CP and the NUWM. After Gaitskell spoke on the same platform as local communists, the right wing of the local Labour Party passed a resolution to reject any united front work against fascism. Gaitskell was banned from speaking in future on the same platform as communists. Three prominent local Labour Party members resigned from the party in protest.[235]

In Wales it was the miners' lodges and the CP who were central to organising anti-fascist protests. Following the initial anti-fascist protests in Wales a conference was organised at Pontypridd Town Hall in April 1936. Representatives from ten Rhondda miners' lodges, the CP, the NUWM, Pontypridd Trades and Labour Council, and the miners' Cambrian Combine Committee met. They resolved to unite in action against Mosley in Wales.[236]

Throughout 1936 Mosley drew inspiration from the strength of the Nazi regime in Germany, and the war on democracy launched by the fascist general Franco in Spain. In Austria, Hitler approved an agreement that strengthened his control of the country.[237] These fascist advances on the continent drove anti-fascists resolve in Britain.

Tonypandy, Wales, June 1936

In June thousands were mobilised against a BUF meeting with Tommy Moran. News of the planned meeting had got out and a party of Trealaw socialists from the Rhondda had "toured the district during the day announcing a protest demonstration".[238] The BUF rally in Tonypandy at De Winton Fields was broken up after 5,000 to 6,000 anti-fascists gathered to stop the meeting going ahead: "Annie Powell, Britain's first Communist mayor, recalled years later 'we swore not even one Welsh sheep would hear the Mosley message'." It was "the Blackshirts' last act in Wales".[239]

Thirty-seven anti-fascists were arrested that day; most were CP members. The police charged them with offences including riot and incitement to riot. Seven received prison sentences ranging from two to twelve months, and nine were sentenced to twenty days hard labour at what remains the largest trial of anti-fascists to take place anywhere in Britain.[240]

Manchester, June 1936: Blackshirts driven out of Stevenson Square

The BUF held weekly outdoor meetings in Stevenson Square in Manchester's city centre, as well as in Miles Platting, Alexandra Park, and Platt Fields. Where fascist literature was handed out, hatred and incitement against Jews followed. Local communists and youths attempted to drive these fascists off the streets and stop BUF newspaper sellers. Bernard McKenna recalled:

> I remember selling the *Daily Worker* in Oldham Street on Saturday evenings while the Blackshirts were selling their paper opposite. There were quite a few run-ins between the two groups, which often ended in fights. It got quite nasty but in the end we drove them from that part of the city altogether.[241]

This took two years to achieve: "Time and again the fascists only got out of Stevenson Square with a whole skin as a result of quick mobilisation of the police force."[242] One Sunday afternoon a mass mobilisation of workers drove them out of the square. When the BUF returned with increased forces "hundreds of workers taking up cudgels and standing no nonsense drove the fascists off Oldham Street".[243]

When in June Mosley returned to speak in Manchester he was "confronted by a 3,000-strong crowd" out to oppose what was his last big Manchester rally.[244] McKenna was there. He recalled:

> I remember Mosley speaking at the Town Hall. He was just about to start his meeting when thousands of anti-fascists turned up to stop him. The hall was completely surrounded. People were throwing bottles and stones and fireworks and there was a big fight outside the front hall, which went on for quite some time. Mosley had to be smuggled out the back door of the hall by police. As he tried to leave the hall, his car was attacked and people threw stones at him. The police had to charge the crowd to rescue him.
>
> A section of the crowd followed Mosley to his local headquarters in Tomlinson Street and surrounded the building.

People were throwing stones at the windows and the Blackshirt flag was torn down and set alight. I could see Mosley and his lieutenants scurrying around inside the house like trapped rats and it looked like he'd be in serious trouble but the police arrived in the nick of time and they managed to push the crowd away.[245]

Hull, July 1936

Held on a Sunday night the Mosley rally in Hull attracted an estimated crowd of 10,000 people, "the majority there to voice their opposition to Mosley and his political beliefs".[246] As one account reports:

> The size of the crowd was probably no surprise despite the non-stop heavy rain that night. Trade union membership was soaring at the time… Anti-fascist sentiment was rife, not least among the thousands of dockers and railway workers in the city. A small branch of the Communist Party was also active in Hull at the time.

One of Mosley's Hull-based Blackshirts, John Charnley, gave an eyewitness account of what happened: "The trouble which developed and the size of the opposition that had assembled there before our arrival was absolutely beyond our comprehension. It was obvious before the meeting started that there was going to be serious trouble." The *Hull Daily Mail*'s coverage of the rally records BUF members marching down Park Street into Corporation Field in military fashion to the sound of beating drums:

> A few minutes before eight, Sir Oswald arrived, complete with bodyguard. He was bareheaded and wore only a black-shirt uniform. Fascists saluted and a babel of jeers greeted him.

Although a system of loudspeakers had been installed during the afternoon, when Mosley started to speak his microphone failed to work. By now, bricks and stones were starting to fly through the air along with the sound of whistles and cat-calls. After a brick went flying past his head and crashed into a wall behind him, Mosley berated the crowd, claiming "Red hooligans" were responsible for causing the trouble.

With his microphone still not working and the barrage of missiles getting heavier, he eventually gave up. By now, hand-to-hand fighting was taking place between some of the crowd and BUF supporters, some of the latter using their belts to strike out. The Blackshirts then reformed and marched back towards Park Street bridge again with banners flying and drums beating followed by Mosley and his bodyguard in their car. As the car approached the bridge one of its side windows was smashed.

According to the *Mail*, the violence continued on the bridge: "The fascists marched complete with leader, band and banners from the Corporation Field. Shouting and jeering, the crowd followed and surged over Park Street bridge, completely blocking the road and sidewalks."[247] Militant mass protests drove Mosley out of Hull.

Leeds, September 1936

The BUF planned to march through the Leylands Jewish quarter of Leeds, but were banned from doing so by the Leeds City Watch Committee. But "the night before the event many Jewish shops were targeted with swastikas and anti-semitic acts of vandalism".[248]

The next day, 27 September, a thousand fascists met in the centre of Leeds on Calverley Street. They were joined by Mosley and marched up through the town for a final BUF rally at

Holbeck Moor. They were met by 30,000 protesters led by the Leeds Communist Party.[249] Police helped the BUF hold their rally on Holbeck Moor. The speeches took place around a van which Mosley climbed on top of to speak to the crowd:

> Protesters surrounded the van and sang the Red Flag in order to drown out Mosley's speech and many threw stones at the fascists. Mosley was reportedly dodging stones while speaking to the crowd. The excitement and danger grew as the police started to arrest protesters who were throwing stones, Mosley continued to speak during the confrontation. Finally, the fascists, knowing that they were greatly outnumbered, retreated with great difficulty from Holbeck Moor, with forty fascists being injured from the stones, including their leader Oswald Mosley who was hit in the temple by a large stone. The injured fascists were treated in St Matthew's School next to Holbeck Moor.[250]

Mosley was driven out of Leeds.

The Battle of Cable Street, October 1936

Mosley had been confronted by militant, mass protests in Wales, Manchester, Hull and Leeds. By the end of the year the focus for Mosley and his fascists was the capital city. In London Mosley believed the Metropolitan Police force would be prepared and capable of protecting him and his fascists. He announced the BUF would hold four meetings in the East End, and then a march through the centre of the Jewish community.[251] This brought fear, outrage and anger. It was the "ILP who played an important role opposing Oswald Mosley and the BUF" at Cable Street on Sunday 4 October.[252] "Three days before the demonstration the ILP hired loudspeakers and toured the streets of the East London calling on people to come in their thousands to block all entry points to the East End on Sunday."[253]

The CP had been at the forefront of organising opposition to the Mosley rally in Hyde Park in 1934 when they led mass protests that saw the fascists "drowned by a sea of working-class solidarity". But the political line of the CP had changed in the summer of 1935. At a congress of the Comintern held in Moscow Communist Party leaders agreed the move to a 'Popular Front' policy.

The London YCL had been organising a rally in Trafalgar Square in central London to take place on 4 October in support of Spanish workers. This was same day that Mosley said he would be meeting in the East End. The CP leadership's view was that "Spain was more important than Mosley".[254]

But it was the Labour Party the CP was most focused on: "The Labour Party Conference was about to begin, and the CP hoped to win it to a formal Popular Front".[255] The Labour Party leadership was opposed to a confrontation with the fascists. The CP's leadership feared a mass confrontation with Mosely's Blackshrts in the East End could put the goal of winning Labour to a Popular Front at risk.

The new Popular Front line meant the CP's "politics demanded that they appear 'respectable' at the same time that their members in East London wished to fight the fascists".[256] The CP leadership's Popular Front policy undermined the mobilisation at Cable Street. (Why the Popular Front was introduced, and how it derailed antifascist struggles in France and Spain will be discussed in the chapter).

A call was sent out by the London District of the CP for workers to go in their thousands to Trafalgar Square. Leaflets were printed for the rally, and the *Daily Worker* on Friday 2 October called upon all workers to rally at the Embankment at 2.30pm on Sunday. The line to not support the mobilisation to stop Mosley caused furious arguments in the Stepney branch of the CP. The 24-year-old CP member Joe Jacobs was the secretary of the Stepney branch. He argued that "the best way to help the Spanish people was to stop Mosley marching through the East London. It was the same fight".[257] Such arguments were rebuffed. While the line was held by the London District CP leadership "many CP members were rejecting the Party line in practice".[258]

On Saturday 3 October, the day before the BUF march was due, the ILP call for people to fill the streets in their hundreds of thousands was featured on the front page of the most popular London newspaper, *The Star*. Every newsagent in the East End had a poster for the edition outside reading 'ILP Calls on Workers to Stop Mosley'.[259]

Under pressure from their own members, and with the realisation that the mobilisation to stop Mosley was gaining momentum, the CP leadership changed their line. On the eve of the battle, the call went out "for all branches to rally at Aldgate instead of Trafalgar Square".[260] Walls and pavements were already whitewashed with 'Thou Shall Not Pass!' and 'Bar the road to fascism!' Now the CP gave full official backing for the mobilisation to stop Mosley. The leaflets they had already printed for the Trafalgar Square rally were over-stamped with "Alteration! Rally Aldgate 2pm". Thousands were handed out calling on workers to rally and stop the fascist march.[261] The ILP and the CP commenced the preparations for a vast counter demonstration "to put an end to fascist provocation and terror".[262] The London docker Jack Dash recalls how the East End responded:

> Throughout the night the Stepney folks Jew and Gentile from all walks of life – dockers, stevedores, tailors, engineers, ship repairers, council workers, busmen, railwaymen … with their wives and kids were busy lugging and hauling old furniture, bed springs, tables and chest of draws out on to the streets building barricades. They used anything they could lay their hands on, packing cases, old fish boxes which found their way from nearby Billingsgate fish market … when Sunday dawned Stepney was ready to prevent the fascist march.[263]

To ensure the BUF march could succeed every police officer was on duty. There were 6,000 foot police and a whole mounted division. After the police came the fascists, bussed in on coaches from all parts of London. "The moment the fascists and the police made a turn into Cable Street the signal went out and the barricades went up, a lorry turned over, furniture and wood piled high." A huge crowd blocked the road, with "orthodox Jews and rough and ready Irish Catholic dockers" standing together.[264] As the police charged, they were met with milk bottles, stones and marbles.

When Mosley arrived in his car, a brick went clean through the window.[265] After hours of struggle and resistance, Sir Philip Game, the police commissioner in charge on the day told Mosley it was all over. The fascist march was called off!

Soon after the ILP published a pamphlet *They Did NOT Pass: 300,000 workers Say NO To Mosley*. Celebrating the victory, it explained how "in Germany, Italy, Austria and Spain Fascism has revealed itself as a reign of terror against the workers" but in Britain in the East End workers did not "accept that".[266] For Mussolini in Rome "Cable Street was viewed as a defeat" for the fascist movement, and donations to Mosley's party were suspended.[267] Despite massive police power and numbers, after hours of protest against the police and the BUF, Mosley had been stopped – he was made to turn back. They did not pass! The whole of the East End had mobilised, stopped Mosley, and won. The Battle of Cable Street was the apex of the mass anti-fascist protests that stopped the advance of fascism in Britain.

Driven out of Liverpool, October 1936

Outside of London the strength of the anti-fascist movement was again demonstrated when, one week after Cable Street, the police gave the BUF permission to hold a military-style march in Liverpool. Though the BUF had faced no organised opposition to its first rally in the city in 1933, by 1934 a "local Anti-Fascist Committee had been formed" made up of "Communist Party and Independent Labour Party members, local branches of the National Unemployment Workers' Movement, and some members of the Labour Party". In 1935 the BUF organised smaller meetings, where their "'fascist armoured vans doubled as speaker's platforms". In Bootle a "crowd chased the van to the fascist headquarters on Strand Road, where every window was put in".[268]

On Saturday 11 October 1936, three hundred Blackshirts assembled in full uniform near the Adelphi Hotel by the railway station in the centre of the city, ready to march with Mosley for a BUF rally at the Stadium, a popular boxing venue. Huge crowds mobilised along Lime Street in the centre of Liverpool to oppose the fascist march. Fighting broke out when a fascist armoured van knocked over an elderly man and mounted police were sent in.

Mosley had intended to take the fascist salute at Lime Street and lead the march but the strength of opposition prevented this, so he went direct to the Stadium by car.[269] "All along the march route the fascists were attacked by a constant hail of bricks. At least one was knocked out and had to be carried. Many attempts were made to break into the column. At Lime Street, St John's Lane, Whitechapel, Exchange Street East, and at the Stadium anti-fascists tried to stop the march." The police protected the BUF marchers and secured the area around the Stadium for the fascist rally, "dispersing the gathering crowd after individual Blackshirts were booed".[270] After the meeting the coaches carrying the departing fascists were attacked with bricks and bottles. Mosley was driven out of Liverpool.

Chapter 7
Blackshirt Bye Bye

Organised by local committees, the anti-fascist protests against Mosley throughout 1936 were bigger and more confrontational. It was these mass protests that stopped Oswald Mosley building a strong fascist force in Britain. His plan to lead a fascist Britain failed. One of Britain's leading post-war anti-fascist activists Julie Waterson points out that it "may have worked if it was not for the 'destructive communism' that Mosley's fascism had set out to crush". It was the very 'class warriors from Jerusalem' that Mosley had derided and dismissed at his first public meeting who organised and stopped him and his fascists.[271]

Mosley had seen his meetings disrupted and his speeches drowned out, his outdoor rallies surrounded and the speaker platforms upturned. His *Blackshirt* paper sellers were harassed and pushed out. The hard-core thugs of the Fascist Defence Force were repeatedly beaten back. His marches were disrupted. Mosley was completely blocked at Cable Street. Mosley's fascist movement was effectively smashed. Mass protests had stopped him being able to show "the directness of purpose and energy of method" that Lord Rothermere said would be needed in a British dictator.

What if Mosley had been unopposed? An unopposed Mosley would have strengthened the core of his party, the thugs of the Fascist Defence Force, unleashed to attack Jews more freely and openly. With antisemitism unchallenged and unopposed, division in the working class would have increased, with a divided class less able to fight back and defend their own interests and living standards. The mass anti-fascist struggles across the country in 1934, and throughout 1936, and finally the battle of Cable Street showed the how effective, united, mass mobilisations were in stopping fascists from meeting, organising and marching on the streets.

The turn in the Comintern: the Popular Front replaces the United Front

The CP policy of active opposition to the fascist Mosley in Britain was short-lived. For Stalin and the Comintern the 'united front' policy they had declared after Hitler destroyed the German Communist Party was a brief episode, one of Stalin's many political "zig zags".[272] Now the new policy was for a 'People's Front', with the task for communists to build what was called a 'Popular Front'. The change was first agreed at a meeting of the Comintern in the summer of 1935. The Popular Front policy meant that building political alliances between the Russian state and western governments would now be more important than building militant anti-fascist protests, or leading strikes. The priority for Stalin was making trade deals with Britain and establishing contacts between Russian and French diplomats. Militant resistance to the fascists was replaced by widespread condemnation of fascism, while building an alliance with liberal politicians and parties.

The Popular Front in France and Spain

In France and Spain popular opposition to fascism led to the election in 1936 of 'Popular Front' governments, but the growing radicalisation of the working class meant that workers wanted to go beyond the limited programmes of the very governments they had elected. In both France and

Spain, the policy of supporting Popular Front governments would bring "communists into opposition with the workers' revolutionary strivings on a national scale".[273]

Popular Front in France

In France in February 1934, "the far right had hopes of emulating Hitler's victory of a year before". On 6 February, fascists groups organised a huge demonstration against the recently formed left of centre government. Their aim was to "invade the Chamber of Deputies" and force a "replacement rightwing government so opening the door to power for themselves".[274] The demonstration left 15 dead and hundreds wounded. The prime minster resigned the next day and was replaced by a more right wing figure.

In response to this fascist attempt at a coup, the major union federation the CGT called a general strike for 12 February. The Socialist Party called a demonstration. Then the Communists decided to demonstrate as well, but "separately from the others organisations".[275] Although the communists and socialists were divided and had organised separate anti-fascist demonstrations, on the day "as they drew closer together, people began chanting the same anti-fascist slogans and melted into a single demonstration".[276] In "one unforgettable moment the two columns joined together to cries of Unity! Unity! For the first time in years the socialists and communists were marching side by side".[277]

"The success of the general strike and the united demonstration halted the right's advance" in France and gave confidence to the workers and the left. An electoral pact between the Communists and Socialists was formed. However, it was then extended to the Radicals, a bourgeois pro-capitalist party with liberal politics. In May 1936, a "Popular Front of

Socialist and Communists and Radicals" gained a clear majority in the elections and took office, just as "the biggest strike wave France had ever known" was growing. The employers were forced to make concessions; they offered wage contracts, big wage rises, holiday pay, and a the forty-hour week.

But "among the workers there was a feeling that they wanted something more. They wanted somehow to change society in its entirety". But the French CP leaders declared, "one must know when to end a strike".[278] They used the control they now had of the largest trade union in France, the CGT, which had called the anti-fascist strike of 1934, to successfully de-mobilise what was becoming a pre-revolutionary situation in 1936.

The popular front policy was brought about by the French Communist Party and the Comintern as part of Russia's foreign policy. "Stalin wanted an alliance with France and Britain against Nazi Germany, and the Popular Front was intended to aid this. The Popular Front would see to it that the Communist Parties would be reliable allies in a war of national defence" of the Russian state.[279] For Stalin the signing of a bilateral military treaty with France was paramount.[280] Revolutionary change was no longer supported by the Communists in Russia. Fascism would be beaten by diplomacy and treaties, not mass resistance and strikes.

By 1937, the Popular Front government, which the Communist Party backed, was in crisis, cutting public spending and moving to the right. In March, police opened fire on an anti-fascist demonstration in Clichy, a suburb of Paris, killing six. In 1938 the Popular Front was attacking one the key gains of 1936, the forty hour week. By the end of 1938 it was effectively finished. In 1940, the parliament elected on a wave of hope and enthusiasm in 1936 "voted to give dictatorial powers to Marshal Pétain, who formed a government containing French fascists to collaborate with the German Nazis in occupation of the northern half of the country".[281] The Popular Front strategy in France did not stop fascism.

Popular Front in Spain

It was a similar story in Spain. In 1936 a Popular Front of communists, socialists and liberal pro-capitalist parties won a general election and elected a Republican government. The result gave working class people the confidence to fight for more, with a wave of strikes, occupations and demonstrations. But it also led to a conservative-backed coup led by general Franco who, with backing from part of the Spanish army, the upper classes and the Catholic church wanted to end the country's experiment in democracy and social reform. Franco's forces conducted a brutal civil war.

It was revolutionary action by workers that halted the takeover by Franco's forces. They armed themselves, took over army barracks and convinced soldiers to join them. Anti-fascist committees organised security and supplies, occupied buildings were converted into people's restaurants, hospitals or schools. When the author George Orwell arrived in Spain in 1936, he described Barcelona as a city with "workers in the saddle", in what he believed now was "really a workers' state."[282]

As the Spanish Civil War developed the Republicans struggled to hold back the advance of Franco's well-armed forces which were backed by Hitler and Mussolini. A call was issued for volunteers to join military units to fight on the Republican side against Franco. Many of the best working class anti-fascists from Britain and around the world volunteered; they joined the International Brigades and went to fight against fascism in Spain.[283]

Throughout the summer of 1936 the anti-fascists in Manchester continued to mobilise against Mosley and the BUF. But now building support for the Republicans fighting Franco in Spain became more pressing. The Challenge Club started weekly street collections for food and money – Aid for Spain.

Chapter 8
Anti-fascists after Cable Street

When the call was made for volunteers to fight in Spain many applied to go. Maurice Levine joined the International Brigades and went to Spain to fight. On his return he wrote, *Cheetham to Cordova: A Manchester Man of the Thirties.*[284]

> On 22nd November I left Manchester with Bill Benson, Eddie Swindles and three Jewish lads from north Manchester; Ralph Cantor, Jud Colman, and George Westfield. All three were killed fighting in Spain. I didn't tell my parents I was going. I had arranged with a girl I was friendly with, whom I eventually married, to get in touch with my family and tell them. So I was already on my way to Spain when they heard about it. They never remonstrated with me. I firmly believe my father was quite proud his son had gone to fight; the received wisdom that 'Jews were not fighting people' was proved wrong.[285]

Evelyn Taylor went into Europe and "worked with the communist underground running guns to the anti-fascist fighters in the underground movements against Nazi and fascist dictatorships in Germany, Hungary, Czechoslovakia and Italy".[286] In 1937 she married fellow CP member George Brown but six months later he was killed at the Battle of Brunete. In Spain she met and later married Jack Jones, an International Brigader from Manchester. After the war both Taylor and Jones joined the Labour Party. Jones later became leader of the transport union, the TGWU.[287]

Bernard McKenna joined the ILP's International Brigade as a signaller.[288] He was wounded, captured and imprisoned by the Nazis. McKenna survived and returned home to Manchester. After the Second World War, he joined the Labour Party, but left over the Iraq War and joined the Manchester Socialist Workers Party branch. McKenna was one of the last surviving of the British volunteers who fought in Spain.

The thousands who joined the International Brigades went to fight fascism in Spain. For Stalin however support for the International Brigades was shaped by his wider Popular Front policy. Stalin used the International Brigades to both win alliances with Western governments and maintain his influence in the international labour movement.[289] The International Brigades were organised, financed and armed by Stalin, so he was able to reassure Western governments that Russia was not backing a revolutionary movement in Spain. The struggle would be limited to the 'defence of democracy', and the maintenance of the elected Popular Front government. To enforce this, Stalinists used the repressive apparatus of the Spanish state to suppress those fighting for revolutionary change, by withholding weapons and using spies to locate, imprison, even murder opponents. The supporters of the revolution were attacked in the name of 'unity' of the Popular Front government. They argued that "the revolution should be put on hold in order to concentrate on the defeat of Franco" and "let us finish Franco first and make the revolution afterward".[290]

George Orwell was, initially, sympathetic to this position.[291] However, his application in Britain to join the International Brigades had been blocked by Pollitt. The leader of the CP regarded Orwell as unreliable. So instead, on arrival in Spain Orwell joined the POUM's militia.[292]

His wife Eileen O'Shaughnessy joined him. She worked at the POUM headquarters "on print and radio propaganda for the party, provisioning the men, dealing with communications, arranging the transport of medical supplies".[293] The POUM were fighting Franco's fascist forces as well as attempting to drive forward the revolutionary process. They were independent of the Communists. Subsequently when the CP moved to suppress the POUM, Orwell had to flee for his life. If he had stayed, he believed he would certainly "have had a bullet in the back for being 'politically unreliable', that or jail".[294] The Stalinists suppression of the revolutionary upsurge in 1936-37, far from strengthening the Republic's military front, decisively weakened it and opened a path for the eventual victory of Franco's fascists in April 1939. Once again, the Popular Front strategy had failed.

Popular Front in Britain

In France the Popular Front policy led to the CP shutting down a revolutionary wave of strikes. In Spain it ended with communists butchering a revolution that could have stopped the fascists. What was the result of the Popular Front policy in Britain?[295] For the CP the Popular Front policy led to a move away from militant anti-fascist protests, and the building of alliances with more moderate liberal forces, and the re-writing of the CP's militant anti-fascist history.

A united front of anti-fascist resistance prevailed at Battle of Cable Street, if only after a last minute U-turn by the CP. But after Cable Street, far from drawing the lessons of that victory, the CP's Popular Front line saw the party continue to draw back from mass mobilisation and physical confrontation with Mosley's BUF. Instead, the CP leadership counterposed this approach to a broader anti-fascist Popular Front with more 'respectable' forces, including wings of the British establishment.

Some were for reaching out even to 'anti-fascist' supporters of Winston Churchill. Although Churchill had been a supporter of Italian fascism, after Italy conquered Abyssinia, and Hitler increased arms spending and built up German military forces, Churchill saw the fascist states as a growing threat to British interests. Churchill was not opposed to 'fascism', he was opposed to a challenge to the British Empire by the German fascist state.[296] "Many Labour and trades union stalwarts who supported the working class united front strategy thought that the people's front meant dropping socialist aims, and were too suspicious of liberals, let alone dissident Conservatives and Churchill's followers to go the whole way to an alliance of all anti-fascists."[297] To be effective in the Popular Front policy of uniting with more establishment political forces past confrontations and the militancy of anti-fascist mobilisations were downplayed or erased from history.[298]

Phil Piratin was a Stepney branch CP member active at the Battle of Cable Street. When he stood for election as a CP candidate, the history of anti-fascist struggles in the East End aided his campaign. As a "result of 15 years of campaigning on fundamentally working class issues" Piratin was elected in 1945 as the CP Member of Parliament for the Mile End constituency.[299] In 1948 Piratin wrote the influential and much quoted book about the battle with the BUF in the East End, *Our Flag Stays Red*. He states clearly that he wrote this book to aid the CP campaign for the London Council elections where Piratin was one of candidates.[300] For Piratin it was rent strikes that were the key to beating back the BUF, rather than the confrontational united action against the BUF at Cable Street. Rent strikes were led by

CP members. Two years after Cable Street "in 1938 tenants at two large East End Estates held bitter rent strikes simultaneously, which lasted for months".[301] United action over the cost of living, rent strikes, fights over low pay, against unemployment – all demonstrate how our class can unite and fight back. It can erode some fascist support. Such struggles can, potentially, give greater confidence and organisation to anti-fascists. But fascism does not simply disappear when workers unite and fight back of economic and social questions, if the fascists are not also directly targeted, isolated and confronted. Mass strikes and struggles by French workers did not stop the fascists growing in the 1930s.[302] Fascists must be directly challenged and confronted to be beaten.

Piratin criticised those in the Stepney branch of the CP for what he calls their "bash the fascist whenever you see them" practice.[303] But as Joe Jacobs recalled:

> The questions really being asked at that time were, how do we meet the growing attacks on individual Jews who were being violently assaulted by fascists and how do we meet the growing assault on our organised activity? What do we do when our people were whitewashing and selling papers and we're attacked by a Mosley force? How do we stop them gaining further support from workers vulnerable to antisemitic propaganda?[304]

For advocating the continuation of anti-fascist defence the CP leadership expelled Jacobs from the party. Mosley and the BUF did not stop their attacks after Cable Street but the CP did become more hesitant and cautious in its approach to stopping the BUF.[305]

By 1937 Mosley's fascist organisation had been significantly weakened. A few BUF branches remained, confined to London's East End. Mosley had lost the support he once enjoyed from business leaders, media barons, and royals. His Fascist Defence Force lost its funding after money from Mussolini was cut following Mosley's defeat at Cable Street. And while once Churchill had once been an admirer of Mussolini's fascist politics, now Britain's rulers saw fascist Italy and Nazi Germany increasingly as a threat to British interests, a challenge to the British Empire. The BUF were potential 'fifth columnists' once war was declared in 1939.[306]

However, in 1937 in an attempt to revive its fortunes, the BUF did make attempts to march – in Southampton, Liverpool and south London – only to be smashed once again. But the CP, once the driving force of the anti-fascist movement, played a much more inconsistent role in these final confrontations with Mosley's forces.

Southampton, July 1937

On 18 July, 1937, BUF organised a march through the centre of Southampton to the Common, where Mosley spoke from on top of a loud speaker van, "surrounded by his black shirted bodyguards".[307] A huge crowd contained a sizeable core of anti-fascists who drowned out Mosley:

> On the day itself between 15,000 and 20,000 people, including perhaps 4,000 organised anti-fascists, 'gathered round the black loud speaker van from which Sir Oswald spoke'. From the outset… Mosley 'was greeted with "boos" and catcalls from a section of the crowd, and a few missiles were thrown'. Mosley spoke for 45 minutes, but throughout that time the increasingly hostile crowd 'shouted and sang, keeping the chorus up for sometime 'We Don't Want Mosley'. Indeed, Mosley's words 'had not been heard by more than a handful of supporters'.[308]

Some accounts then suggest Mosley tried to escape in an empty tram car but a window was smashed and the trams' electrics were pulled apart, forcing him to flee.[309]

According one history of these events, the CP was not the driving force of the anti-fascist mobilisation: "the Communist Party had arranged a meeting on the same day in a different part of The Common. The slim coverage in the *Daily Worker* could suggest that the Communist Party were unimpressed with the demonstration."[310]

Bermondsey, October 1937

The BUF had no local branch in Bermondsey, but it held a number of marches in the area as it sought to recover lost momentum. The largest of these marches was on 3 October and became known as 'the battle of Bermondsey'.[312] "Mosley's supporters assembled near Millbank... Some 3,000 marchers formed up three abreast in a procession, convoyed by 30 mounted police at the front, and busloads of foot police bringing up the rear; 'one policeman for every fascist marcher', the *Daily Mirror* remarked."[313] "Bermondsey had a strong left wing tradition, based on active local trade unionism among dockers and factory workers, linked to an active branch of the Independent Labour party; Bermondsey Borough's local council was run by a leftwing Labour administration."[314]

It was Bermondsey Trades Council who called the massive counter-demo: "they were supported by the Communist Party and Independent Labour Party – although the CP in fact were not keen on militant opposition at this point, but were forced by the actions of the Trades Council and local feeling to back the call."[315] Just as at Cable Street, the fascist march to Bermondsey was to be prevented from reaching its end point by barricades built by thousands of anti-fascists. In Bermondsey, the 'Popular Front' approach from the CP was challenged by a 'united front' of opposition from trades unionists and anti fascists.

Liverpool, October 1937

A week after the events in Bermondsey, the BUF organised a rally in Walton, Liverpool on 10 October with Mosely due to speak from the top of a loud hailer van:

> An hour before Mosley was due to speak the Communist Party had already organised a public meeting on the same piece of ground. By the time the fascist armoured van arrived, the police had to clear a way through a hostile crowd of 10,000. When an electrician started to erect a microphone on the van roof, cries of 'Down with Mosley' and 'We don't want fascism here' changed to volleys of bricks and stones - smashing the van's windscreen... Mosley arrived soon after by car and climbed onto the van. After giving the fascist salute, and before he'd spoken, he was also dropped, by a stone hitting his left temple. Lying on the van roof, he was hit again, on the back of the head, and knocked unconscious. Mounted police immediately moved in and attacked the crowd, clearing the area.[311]

Mosley had to be treated in Walton hospital. It was his last public event in Liverpool.

Remembering, not forgetting, the past

The CP historians in the post Second World War period wrote many important and influential works, on the development of capitalism, the growth of industry and empire, and the history of the workers movement. Among the members of the influential Communist Party Historians Group[316] were E.P. Thompson, Dorothy Thompson, Christopher Hill, Eric Hobsbawm, John Saville, and Maurice Dobb.[317] "The group were part of a generation shaped by the experience of the 1930s". E.P. Thompson "was radicalised by the depression of the 1930s and the rise of the Nazis", he believed it was necessary to "place our bodies between fascism and freedom".[318] However, the CP Historians Group had agreed with the CP leadership that "they would not touch the history of the British Labour movement in the twentieth century".[319] As Hobsbawm explained, this was because it would mean confronting the role of the CP leadership since its formation in 1920, which would have "raised some notoriously tricky problems".[320] So no CP historian wrote about the young communists in Britain who led the struggle in which many workers did put 'their bodies on the line' fighting against the fascist Mosley.

By drawing extensively on reports in local papers and archives, along with interviews and testimonies of those anti-fascists who took part, I have constructed a history that shows how a series of mass anti-fascist struggles stopped Mosley delivering on his promise to demonstrate the BUF's ability to stand up to 'communist disorder'. I hope the history I have written here is a fitting tribute, worthy of the courage and determination of those who beat back Mosley. In Britain we have a political tradition of fighting fascism by uniting in action against them. This is a tradition to build upon, to inspire and guide us in our own fight against racism and fascism today.

The fight against Mosley was led by young CP members out to stop the spread of fascism across Europe. They wanted a better world. Many joined the CP seeking a revolutionary transformation of society akin to the change in Russia which saw the "forceable entrance of the masses into the realm of rulership over their own destiny".[321] From the late 1920s, the leadership of the CP however followed the line put by the counter-revolutionary Stalin in Russia where those who had led the revolution of 1917 were subject to show trials, liquidation and murder.[322]

It was Leon Trotsky who provided an alternative political leadership to Stalin. Trotsky kept alive the revolutionary tradition. From exile he spelt out the danger from fascist forces and how they could be stopped using the political tactic of building a united front. This method was based on the united fight that stopped the 'would be fascist' general Kornilov in August 1917. Following the defeat of Kornilov's counter revolutionary forces, Trotsky, Lenin and the Bolshevik party went on to lead a revolution that completely transformed Russia. The October revolution inspired a generation across the world seeking hope and systemic change. The political challenge for anti-fascists and revolutionary socialists today is to not only hold back and defeat fascism, but also to build socialist organisation that fights for a revolutionary transformation of society.

Bibliography

Primary sources

People's History Museum (PHM) Archive, Box 1/193. The PHM houses the Labour Party national archives. Their collection includes a cut and paste scrap book of press cuttings, reports, and letters of all that was associated with Oswald Mosley and the BUF.

Books and articles

Ali, Tariq. 2022, *Winston Churchill: His Times and Crimes* (Verso).

Ashman, Sam, 1998, "The Communist Party Historians Group" in Rees, John (ed.), *Essays on Historical Materialism* (Bookmarks).

Balfour, Arthur, 1905, *Hansard;* https://api.parliament.uk/historic-hansard/commons/1905/ may/02/ aliens-bill-1

Barlow, Nigel, 2024, "Chaim Weizmann – The Manchester man behind the founding of Israel", https://aboutmanchester.co.uk/chaim-weizmann-the-manchester-man-behind-the-founding-of-israel/

Basketter, Simon, 2013, "The Comintern: a beacon for world revolution', *Socialist Worker*, issue 2353; https://socialistworker.co.uk/features/the-comintern-a-beacon-for-world-revolution/

Basketter, Simon, 2020, "Fighting fascism – remembering the International Brigades", *Socialist Worker*, issue 2727; https://socialistworker.co.uk/features/fighting-fascism-remembering-the-international-brigades/

Basketter, Simon, 2022, "Giorgia Meloni – meet the fascist who could soon lead Italy's government", *Socialist Worker*, issue 2822; https://socialistworker.co.uk/international/giorgia-meloni-meet-the-fascist-who-could-soon-lead-italys-government/

Basketter, Simon, 2023, "Capitalism and the Holocaust", *Socialist Worker*, issue 2839; https:// socialistworker.co.uk/features/capitalism-and-the-holocaust/

Beckman, Morris, 2013, *The 43 Group: Battling with Mosley's Blackshirts* (The History Press).

Beckman, Morris, 2018, "Fighting fascists: Battling Oswald Mosley's Blackshirts", https://thehistorypress.co.uk/article/fighting-fascists-battling-oswald-mosleys-blackshirts/

Beetham, David, 1983, *Marxists in the Face of Fascism* (Manchester University Press).

Behan, Tom, 2003, *The Resistible Rise of Benito Mussolini* (Bookmarks).

Bennett, Theresa, 2002, "The hidden history of Asians in Britain", *Socialist Worker*, Issue 1809; https://socialistworker.co.uk/features/the-hidden-history-of-asians-in-britain/

Bennett, Weyman, 2013, 'Breaking the Fascist Threat' in Richardson, Brian (ed.), *Say it Loud: Marxism and the Fight Against Racism* (Bookmarks).

Boisseau, Will, 2011, "Remembering and Forgetting Anti-Fascism", *History Workshop Journal*; *https://www. historyworkshop.org.uk/anti-fascism/ remembering-and-forgetting-anti-fascism/*

Branson, Noreen, 1985, *History of the Communist Party of Great Britain, 1927–41* (Lawrence and Wishart).

Brossat, Alain, and Klinberg, Sylvie, 2009, *Revolutionary Yiddisherland: A History of Jewish Radicalism* (Verso).

Broué, Pierre, 2006, *The German Revolution 1917-23* (The Merlin Press).

Brown, Geoff, 2025, *A People's History of the Anti Nazi League* (Bookmarks).

Burgon, Richard, 2024, "MP's Notebook: The Battle of Holbeck Moor", *South Leeds Life*; https:// southleedslife.com/mps-notebook-the-battle-of-holbeck-moor/

Callinicos, Alex, 2012, "Julie Waterson (1958-2012): our most fearless fighter", *Socialist Worker*, issue 2330; https://socialistworker.co.uk/ obituaries/julie-waterson-1958-2012-our-most-fearless-fighter/

Callinicos, Alex, 2021, "Neoliberal capitalism implodes: global catastrophe and the far right today", *International Socialism* journal, 170; http://isj.org.uk/implodes-catastrophe/

Callinicos, Alex, 2023, *The New Age of Catastrophe* (Polity).

Cesarani, 1989, "The anti-Jewish career of Sir William Joynson-Hicks, Cabinet Minister", *Journal of Contemporary History*, 24.

Cliff, Tony, 1993, *Trotsky 1927–40: The Darker the Night the Brighter the Star* (Bookmarks).

Cliff, Tony, 2000, *Marxism at the Millennium* (Bookmarks); https:// www.marxists.org/archive/cliff/ works/2000/millennium/chap09.htm

Cliff, Tony, and Gluckstein, Donny, 1986, *Marxism and Trade Union Struggle: The General Strike of 1926* (Bookmarks).

Crowley, Michael, 2022, *Comrades Come Rally! Manchester Communists in the 1930s and 1940s* (Bookmarks).

Cookson, Matthew, 2008, "Labour's 'Great betrayal' led to the brink of collapse", *Socialist Worker*, issue 2103; https://socialistworker.co.uk/features/ labour-s-great-betrayal-led-to-the-brink-of-collapse/

Dawsey, Jason, 2022, "Dachau, the 'Model' Concentration Camp, 1933-39", National World War 2 Museum New Orleans, https:// www.nationalww2museum.org/war/ articles/dachau-model-concentration-camp-1933-39

Danos, Jacques, and Gibelin, Marcel, 1986, *June '36: Class Struggle and the Popular Front in France* (Bookmarks).

Deutscher, Isaac, 1948, "The Economic Policy of the Soviet", *The Listener;* https://www.marxists.org/archive//deutscher/1948/economic-policy.htm

Dorril, Stephen, 2007, *Black Shirt: Sir Oswald Mosley and British Fascism* (Penguin Books).

Englert, Sai, 2012, "The rise and fall of the Jewish Labour Bund", *International Socialism* journal, 135; http://isj.org.uk/the-rise-and-fall-of-the-jewish-labour-bund/

Edelman, Marek, 2013, *The Ghetto Fights: Warsaw 1943-45* (Bookmarks).

Flint, Josh, 2019, "Oswald Mosley and Leeds – The Battle of Holbeck Moor 27th September 1936", (Leeds Libraries); https://secretlibraryleeds.net/2019/06/14/oswald-mosley-and-leeds-the-battle-of-holbeck-moor-27th-september-1936/

Foot, John, 2022, *Blood and Power: The Rise and Fall of Italian Fascism* (Bloomsbury).

Foot, Paul, 1988, "The great times they could have had", *London Review of Books,* Vol.10, No. 16; https://www.lrb.co.uk/the-paper/v10/n16/paul-foot/the-great-times-they-could-have-had

Fighting Talk, 1996, "Stoned by the Mersey: Opposing the Blackshirts in Liverpool", Issue 13; https://libcom.org/article/stoned-mersey-opposing-blackshirts-liverpool

Frow, Ruth and Frow, Edmund, 1978, *The Communist Party in Manchester, 1920-26* (Working Class Movement Library).

Funder, Anna, 2023, *Wifedom: Mrs Orwell's Invisible Life* (Penguin).

Fyrth, Jim (ed.), 1985, *British Fascism and the Popular Front* (Lawrence and Wishart).

Gewirtz, Sharon, 1990, "Anti-fascist activity in Manchester's Jewish Community in the 1930s", *Manchester Region History Review;* https://afaarchive.files.wordpress.com/2012/06/anti-fascist-jews-manchester-1930s.pdf

Gluckstein, Donny, 1999, *The Nazis, Capitalism and the Working Class* (Bookmarks).

Gluckstein, Donny, 2013, "The resistible rise of Adolf Hitler", *Socialist Worker,* issue 2338; https://socialistworker.co.uk/features/the-resistible-rise-of-adolf-hitler/

Gluckstein, Donny and Stone, Janey, 2023, *The Radical Jewish Tradition: Revolutionaries, Resistance Fighters and Firebrands* (Bookmarks).

Gray, Todd, 2006, *Blackshirts in Devon* (The Mint Press).

Groves, Reg, 1974, *The Balham Group: How British Trotskyism Began* (Pluto).

Hallas, Duncan, 1985, *The Comintern* (Bookmarks).

Hallas, Duncan and others, 2023, *Indomitable Revolutionary* (Bookmarks).

Hann, Dave, 2013, *Physical Resistance: A Hundred Years of Anti Fascism* (Zero Books).

Hannington, Wal, 1977, *Unemployed Struggles, 1919-1913* (Lawrence and Wishart).

Hayes, Ali, 2019, "The day Oswald Mosley spoke to 15,000 people at Southampton Common – and was hit by a rock", Southern Daily Echo; https://www.dailyecho.co.uk/news/17462116.day-oswald-mosley-spoke-15-000-people-southampton-common---hit-rock/

Hare, Chris, 1991, *Historic Worthing: The Untold Story* (Windrush Press).

Harman, Chris, 1982, *The Lost Revolution: Germany 1918-1923* (Bookmarks).

Harman, Chris, 1999, *A People's History of the World* (Bookmarks).

Hodgson, Keith, 2010, *Fighting Fascism: The British Left and the Rise of Fascism, 1919-39* (Manchester University Press).

Hogsbjerg, Christian, 2006, "The fascist invasion of Abyssinia", *Socialist Worker,* issue 1998; https://socialistworker.co.uk/features/the-fascist-invasion-of-abyssinia/

Holborow, Paul, 2019, "The Anti Nazi League and its lessons for today", *International Socialism* journal, 163; https://isj.org.uk/the-anti-nazi-league/

Independent Labour Party special pamphlet, 1936, *They Did NOT Pass: 300,000 workers Say NO To Mosley,* https://mrc-catalogue.warwick.ac.uk/records/MSH/2/209/101; *https://www.independentlabour.org.uk/wp-content/uploads/2016/10/They-did-not-pass.pdf*

Isaacs, Harold R., 1938, *The Tragedy of the Chinese Revolution*; https://www.marxists.org/history/ etol/writers/isaacs/1938/tcr/

Jacobs, Joe, 1991, *Out of the Ghetto: My Youth in the East End, Communism and Fascism, 1913-39* (Phoenix Press).

Jewish Voice for Peace, 2017, *On Antisemitism, Solidarity and the Struggle for Justice* (Haymarket).

Jones, Jack, 1986, *Union Man: Autobiography* (Harper Collins).

Keynes, J.M., 1971, *The Collected Writings of John Maynard Keynes: Activities, 1929–1931, Rethinking Employment and Unemployment Policies* (Macmillan).

Kimber, Charlie, 2017, "A colonial massacre in Africa fully revealed for the first time", *Socialist Worker,* issue 2585; https://socialistworker.co.uk/news/a-colonial-massacre-in-africa-fully-revealed-for-the-first-time

Krantz, Mark, 2019, "The long history of Palestine", *International Socialism* journal, 162 https://isj.org.uk/the-long-history-of-palestine/

Levine, Maurice, 1984, *Cheetham to Cordova: A Manchester Man of the Thirties* (Neil Williamson).

Maitles, Henry, 1994, "Blackshirts across the border", *Socialist Review,* 172; http:// pubs.socialistreviewindex.org.uk/sr172/maitles.htm

Malm, Andreas, and the Zetkin Collective, 2021, *White Skin Black Fuel: On the Danger of fossil Fascism* (Verso).

McFarlane, Gary, 2013, "From confrontation to compromise: Black British politics in the 1970s and 1980s", in Richardson, Brian (ed.), *Say it Loud; Marxism and the Fight Against Racism* (Bookmarks).

Miliband, Ralph, 1972, *Parliamentary Socialism: A Study in the Politics of Labour* (Merlin Press).

mudlark121, 2019, "Today in London anti-fascist history, 1937: mass opposition prevents British Union of Fascists marching into Bermondsey", *London Radical Histories; https://pasttense. co.uk/2019/10/03/today-in-london-anti-fascist-history-1937-mass-opposition-prevents-british-union-of-fascists-marching-into-bermondsey/*

Mullally, Frederic, 1946, *Fascism inside England* (Claud Morris).

Newsinger, John, 2018, *Hope Lies in the Proles, George Orwell and the Left* (Pluto Press).

Newsinger, John, 2023, "In the Middle of the Road: Fenner Brockway, the Independent Labour Party and the class struggle", *International Socialism* journal, 179; http://isj.org.uk/fenner-brockway-ilp/

O'Neill, Christina, 2019, "How Govanhill defeated Oswald Mosely's Blackshirts in the 1930s", *Glasgow Live; https://www.glasgowlive.co.uk/ news/glasgow-news/blackshirts-govanhill-oswald-mosley-16787260*

O'Neill, Dan, 2014, "British Fascist leader got short shrift from his Welsh audiences", *Wales Online,* https://www.walesonline.co.uk/ lifestyle/nostalgia/british-fascist-leader-short-shrift-7013581

Orwell, George, 1938, *Homage to Catalonia* (Penguin); https://www. marxists.org/archive/orwell/ 1938/ homage-catalonia.htm

Pappe, Ilan, 2024, *Lobbying for Zionism on both sides of the Atlantic* (One World).

Pollitt, Harry, 1940, *Serving My Time: An Apprenticeship to Politics* (Lawrence & Wishart).

Paxton, Robert O., 2005, *The Anatomy of Fascism* (Penguin).

Pearce, Brian and Woodhouse, Michael, 1995, *A History of Communism in Britain* (Bookmarks).

Pike, Cecil, MP, 1934, "British Union Fascists", *Hansard;* https:// api.parliament.uk/historic-hansard/ commons/1934/jun/26/british-union-of-fascists

Piratin, Phil, 1978 (1948), *Our Flag Stays Red* (Lawrence and Wishart).

Regan, Barnard, 2017, *The Balfour Declaration: Empire, the Mandate and Resistance in Palestine* (Verso).

Rollo, Joanna, 1977, "History of Immigration", *International Socialism* journal, 1st series 96; https://www. marxists.org/history/etol/newspape/ isj/1977/no096/rollo.htm

Rosenberg, Chanie, 1995, *1919: Britain on the Brink of Revolution* (Bookmarks).

Rosenberg, David, 2011, *Battle for the East End: Jewish Responses to Fascism in the 1930s* (Impress Books).

Rosemberg, David, 2019, "On this day – 3 October 1937: the battle of Bermondsey"; https://rebellion602.wordpress.com/2019/10/03/on-this-day-3-october-1937-the-battle-of-bermondsey/

Rothman, Benny, 1994, "The Mosley Rally, Kings Hall Belle Vue, February 1933", *North West Labour History journal*, 18.

Rothman, Benny, 2012, *The Battle for Kinder Scout: Including the 1932 Mass Trespass* (Willow Publishing).

Serdiville, Rosie, 2018, "The Battle of Stockton Campaign", *North East History* 49, pp85-89.

Sewell, Dave, 2017, "Marine Le Pen's front for fascism", *Socialist Worker*, issue 2549; https://socialistworker.co.uk/news/macron-wins-french-presidential-election-but-fascist-threat-has-grown/

Sherry, Dave, 2017, *Russia 1917: Workers' Revolution and the Festival of the Oppressed* (Bookmarks).

Sherry, Dave, 2023, "Stalinism, the United Front and the International Socialist Tradition", in Hallas, Duncan and others, *Indomitable Revolutionary* (Bookmarks).

Simkin, John, 2014, "The notorious Charles Bentinck Budd and the British Union of Fascists", *Sussex World*; https://www.sussexexpress.co.uk/sport/nostalgia/the-notorious-charles-bentinck-budd-and-the-british-union-of-fascists-2269231

Simons, Mike, 2016, *Reminiscences of RAR: Rocking Against Racism, 1976-1982* (Redwords).

Skidelsky, Robert, 1981, *Oswald Mosley* (Macmillan).

Socialist Worker, 2017, "Racism was at the heart of Football Lads Alliance march", issue 2575; https://socialistworker.co.uk/news/racism-was-at-the-heart-of-football-lads-alliance-march/

Sparks, Colin, 1977, "Fighting the Beast: Fascism – The Lessons of Cable Street", *International Socialism* journal, 1st series 94; https://www.marxists.org/history/etol/newspape/isj/1977/no094/sparks.htm

Sparks, Colin, 1978-79, "Masses against Mosley", *Socialist Review* 8; https://www.marxists.org/history/etol/newspape/socrev/1978/sr008/contents.html

Spriano, Paolo, 1975, *The Occupation of the Factories: Italy 1920* (Pluto Press).

Thomas, Mark L., 2023, "Fascism's return to Italy? The meaning of the Fratelli d'Italia", *International Socialism* journal, 178.

Thorpe, Nick, 2022, "Hungary PM Viktor Orban adviser Hegedus resigns over 'pure Nazi' speech", BBC News, https://www.bbc.co.uk/news/world-europe-62313579

Tilles, Daniel, 2015, *British Fascist Antisemitism and Jewish Responses, 1932-40* (Bloomsbury).

Todd, Nigel, 1995, *In Excited Times: The People Against the Blackshirts* (Beswick Press).

Tremlett, Giles, 2021, *The International Brigades: Fascism, Freedom and the Spanish Civil War* (Bloomsbury).

Trotsky, Leon, 1932, *What Next? Vital Questions for the German Proletariat*; https://www.marxists.org/archive/trotsky/germany/1932-ger/next01.htm#s2

Trotsky, Leon, 1974, *The First Five Years of the Communist International* (New Park).

Trotsky, Leon, 1976, *Leon Trotsky on China* (Pathfinder).

Trotsky, Leon, 1979, *History of the Russian Revolution* (Pluto Press).

Trotsky, Leon, 1989, *Fascism, Stalinism and the United Front* (Bookmarks).

Turner, David, 1993, *Fascism and Anti-Fascism in the Medway Towns, 1927-1940* (Kent Anti-Fascist Committee); https://libcom.org/book/export/html/65594

Walsh, David, 2011, "The Battle of Stockton", *Republic of Teesside* blogspot; https://republic-of-teesside.blogspot.com/2011/04/battle-of-stockton.html

Waterson, Julie, 2009, "Mosley's fascists", *Socialist Worker*, issue 2164; https://www.marxists.org/history/etol/writers/waterson/2009/08/mosley.html

West Sussex Record Office, 2019, "Documenting Fascism in 1930s West Sussex"; https://westsussexrecordofficeblog.com/2019/09/20/documenting-fascism-in-1930s-west-sussex/

Williams, Bill, 1988, *Manchester Jewry: A Pictorial History, 1788-1988* (Archive Publications).

Williams, Bill, 2011, *Jews and Other Foreigners: Manchester and the Rescue of the Victims of European Fascism, 1933-1940* (Manchester University Press).

Wincott, Len, 1974, *Invergordon Mutineer* (Littlehampton); https://files.libcom.org/files/Invergordon%20Mutineer.pdf

Young, Angus, 2017, "The Hull race riot involving flying bricks, razor blades in potatoes and a very controversial leader", *Hull Daily Mail*; https://www.hulldailymail.co.uk/news/history/fascist-leader-sir-oswald-mosley-660973

Zetkin, Clara, 2019 [1923], "The Struggle Against Fascism", in Beetham, David (ed.), *Marxists in the Face of Fascism* (Haymarket).

Endnotes

Foreword

1 See Callinicos, Alex, 2012, "Julie Waterson (1958-2012): our most fearless fighter", *Socialist Worker*.

2 Opened in 1932, it closed after Mosley had left Manchester in 1939. The building was sold to an ultra-orthodox Jewish religious group and is now a centre for the Haredi community.

3 Northumberland Street is in Salford, near the border with Manchester.

4 See Piratin, Phil, 1978 [1948], *Our Flag Stays Red*; Jacobs, Joe, 1991, *Out of the Ghetto: My Youth in the East End, Communism and Fascism, 1913-39*; Rosenberg, David, 2011, *Battle for the East End: Jewish Responses to Fascism in the 1930s*.

5 There is a long history of Jewish resistance; see Brossat and Klinberg, 2009, *Revolutionary Yiddisherland: A History of Jewish Radicalism*; Edelman, Marek, 2013, *The Ghetto Fights: Warsaw 1943-45*; Gluckstein, Donny and Stone, Janey, 2023, *The Radical Jewish Tradition: Revolutionaries, Resistance Fighters and Firebrands*.

6 I use the spelling 'antisemitism' rather than 'anti-Semitism'. Although both refer to anti-Jewish sentiment, "the category 'Semite' was imposed by scientific racism, a pseudo-scientific use of scientific techniques and hypotheses to sort humans into different races"; Judith Butler's *foreword* to Jewish Voice for Peace, 2017, *On Antisemitism, Solidarity and the Struggle for Justice*, pxv. The racial meaning of 'anti-Semitism' was first introduced in the late nineteenth century by the German journalist Wilhelm Marr. In his 1862 essay, "The Way to Victory of Germanicism over Judaism", Marr developed a conception of 'anti-Semitism' which focused on the supposed racial, as opposed to religious, characteristics of the Jews. This form of anti-Jewish racism, based on the idea that there is a unique 'Semitic' race, was used by both Hitler and Mosley.

7 Waterson, Julie, 2009, "Mosley's fascists", *Socialist Worker*.

8 Williams, Bill, 1988, *Manchester Jewry: A Pictorial History, 1788-1988*, p97. Salford and Manchester are neighbouring cities.

9 In 1934, the YCL was the youth section of the Communist Party of Great Britain. The CPGB had been established in August 1920. Following the 1989 Eastern European revolutions, the series of uprisings, protests and political crises, that led to the disintegration of the USSR and its satellites, the CPGB dissolved itself in 1991. Thirty years later in Britain in 2021 a group also called the 'YCL' was set up. The politics of this YCL group are an "adulation of Stalin and support for the substantial abuses of state power that occurred under his leadership". See Tomáš Tengely-Evans, 2022, "Stalinism's Long Shadow", *International Socialism* journal *173*.

Introduction

10 Trotsky, Leon, 1989, *Fascism, Stalinism and the United Front.* These writings on fighting fascism were published earlier in the *International Socialism* journal.

11 Sherry, Dave, 2023, "Stalinism, the United Front and the International Socialist Tradition", in Duncan Hallas and others, *Indomitable Revolutionary*, p242.

12 See Holborow, Paul, 2019, "The Anti Nazi League and its lessons for today", *International Socialism* journal.

13 Beckman, Morris, 2013, *The 43 Group: Battling with Mosley's Blackshirts*, p26.

14 Bennett, Weyman, 2013, "Breaking the fascist threat", in Richardson, Brian (ed.), *Say it Loud: Marxism and the Fight Against Racism.*

15 McFarlane, Gary, 2013, "From confrontation to compromise: Black British politics in the 1970s and 1980s", in Richardson, 2013, p88.

16 McFarlane, 2013, p88.

17 See Brown, Geoff, 2025, *A People's History of the Anti Nazi League.*

18 Zetkin, Clara, 2019 [1923], "The Struggle Against Fascism" in Beetham, David (ed.), 2019, *Marxists in the Face of Fascism*, p112.

19 Zetkin, 2019, p112.

20 Trotsky, Leon, 1932, *What Next? Vital Questions for the German Proletariat.*

21 Dorril, Stephen, 2007, *Black Shirt, Sir Oswald Mosley and British Fascism*, p370.

22 Sewell, Dave, 2017, "Marine Le Pen's front for fascism", *Socialist Worker.*

23 Thomas, Mark L., 2023, "Fascism's return to Italy? The meaning of the Fratelli d'Italia", *International Socialism* journal, p20.

24 Thomas, 2023.

25 Basketter, Simon, 2022, "Giorgia Meloni – meet the fascist who could soon lead Italy's government", *Socialist Worker.*

26 Malm, Andreas and the Zetkin Collective, 2021, *White Skin Black Fuel: On the Danger of fossil Fascism*, p92.

27 Thorpe, Nick, 2022, "Hungary PM Viktor Orban adviser Hegedus resigns over 'pure Nazi' speech", BBC News.

28 Callinicos, Alex, 2023, *The New Age of Catastrophe*, p127.

29 Bennett, 2013, p229.

30 Bennett, 2013, p229.

31 Established in 2003, Unite Against Fascism (UAF) "played a central role in challenging and confronting the BNP and the E[nglish] D[efence] L[eague]". See Bennett, 2013, p229 and Richardson 2013, p11.

32 The meaning of 'antisemitism' historically was racism directed against Jewish people, their places of worship, their very existence as Jews. But in 2013 the 'Israeli

lobby' advanced "a new meaning of antisemitism defining anti-semitism to include anti-Zionism and even moderate anti-Israeli stances", Pappe, Ilan, 2024, *Lobbying for Zionism on Both Sides of the Atlantic*, p469.

33 Members of the Communist Party of Great Britain, the CPGB, will be described hereafter as members of the CP.

....

Chapter 1
Fascist forces grow across Europe

34 Spriano, Paolo, 1975, *The Occupation of the Factories: Italy 1920*, p60.

35 Behan, Tom, 2003, *The Resistible Rise of Benito Mussolini*, p39.

36 Foot, John, 2022, *Blood and Power: The Rise and Fall of Italian Fascism*, p38.

37 It is estimated that fascist squads and police attacks killed a total of 6,000 working class people in the period 1917-1922; see Behan, 2003, p111.

38 Ali, Tariq, 2022, *Winston Churchill: His Times and Crimes*, p183.

39 In February 1933 Churchill described Mussolini as the "Roman genius" in a speech at the Queen's Hall in London.

40 Ali, 2022, p184.

41 Gluckstein, Donny, 2013, "The resistible rise of Adolf Hitler", *Socialist Worker*.

42 See Rosenberg, Chanie, 1995, *1919: Britain on the Brink of Revolution*.

43 See Cliff, Tony, and Gluckstein, Donny, 1986, *Marxism and Trade Union Struggle: The General Strike of 1926*.

44 Miliband, Ralph, 1972, *Parliamentary Socialism: A Study in the Politics of Labour*, pp159-181; Cookson, Matthew, 2008, "Labour's 'Great betrayal' led to the brink of collapse", *Socialist Worker*.

45 "Fight The Baby Starvers!" was the slogan on banners carried by Manchester CP members marching against the cuts to benefits.

46 As soon as the cuts to unemployed benefits were made "in Manchester 80,000 unemployed did battle with the police when they attempted to march to the town hall. Mounted police charged repeatedly with their batons, clubbing down old and young. Fire hoses poured tons of water into the crowd. The resistance lasted three hours. Several mounted police officers were dragged from their horses and received punishment from the protesters", Hannington, Wal, 1977, *Unemployed Struggles, 1919-1913*, p226.

47 The National Unemployed Workers Union (NUWM) was organised and led by CP members. See Hannington, 1977.

48 See Wincott, Len, 1974, *Invergordon Mutineer*.

49 Mullally, Frederic, 1946, *Fascism inside England*, p15.

50 Paxton, Robert, O., 2005, *The Anatomy of Fascism*, p75.

51 Keynes, J.M., 1971, *The Collected Writings of John Maynard Keynes: Activities, 1929–1931, Rethinking Employment and Unemployment Policies* (Macmillan), pp473-475.

52 Paxton, 2005, p75.

53 Mullally, 1946, p29.

54 Adjusted by inflation, this is worth £450,000 today.

55 Mullally, 1946, p29.

56 Mullally, 1946, p25.

57 Mullally, 1946, p25.

58 Dorril, 2007, p224.

59 Mullally, 1946, p25.

60 Mullally, 1946, p29.

61 Mullally, 1946, p29. These costs were reported in the *Daily Mail*, 18 January, 1934. The value of £70,000 in 1934 would be over £6.4 million today.

62 Mullally, 1946, p33.

63 Foot, Paul, 1988, "The great times they could have had", *London Review of Books*.

64 O'Neill, Dan, 2014, "British Fascist leader got short shrift from his Welsh audiences", *Wales Online*.

65 Tilles, Daniel, 2015, *British Fascist Antisemitism and Jewish Responses, 1932-40*, p58.

66 Tilles, 2015, p36; Skidelsky, Robert, 1981, *Oswald Mosley*, p353.

67 Tilles, 2015, p34.

68 Tilles, 2015, p63.

Chapter 2
Jewish immigration and antisemitism

69 In 1791, Catherine II ("the Great"), the empress of Russia, authorised the creation of the 'Pale of Settlement', an area in the western part of the empire in which Jewish subjects were required to reside. At its peak, the Pale was home to approximately five million Jews, estimated to be 40 percent of the world's Jewish population at the time. The Russian Revolution led to its abolition in 1917.

70 Yiddish was the language spoken by Ashkenazi Jews in Eastern Europe. The immigrant Jewish community in Manchester and London continued to speak Yiddish.

71 Algemeyner Yiddisher Arbeter Bund in Rusland un Poyln (General Jewish Labour Union in Russia and Poland). See Englert, Sai, 2012, "The rise and fall of the Jewish Labour Bund", *Socialist Worker*.

72 Brossat and Klinberg, 2009, p33.

73 Williams, 1988, p24.

74 Rollo, Joanna, 1977, "History of Immigration", *International Socialism* journal.

75 Williams 1988, p24.

76 In 1917, as the then Tory foreign secretary, Balfour issued the 'Balfour Declaration' that established a 'national home for the Jewish people'. Balfour

opposed Jewish immigration into Britain. He supported limited Jewish immigration to Mandate Palestine, a country then part of the British Empire.

77 Balfour, Arthur, 1905, *Hansard.*

78 Williams, 1988, p97.

79 Gewirtz, Sharon, 1990, "Antifascist activity in Manchester's Jewish Community in the 1930s", *Manchester Region History Review*, p20.

80 Williams, 1988, p97.

81 Levine, Maurice, 1984, *Cheetham to Cordova: A Manchester Man of the Thirties*, p27.

82 Levine, 1984, p26.

83 Known as the 'Board of Deputies', the 'Board of Deputies of British Jews' was established in 1830 to be 'the communal and political leadership of Britain's Jews', Rosenberg, 2011, p13.

84 Branson, Noreen, 1985, *History of the Communist Party of Great Britain, 1927–41*, p113. *Democracy and Dictatorship* was issued on 24 March 1933.

85 Dorrit, 2007, p226.

86 Tilles, 2015, p141.

87 Hodgson, Keith, 2010, *Fighting Fascism: The British Left and the Rise of Fascism 1919–39*, p141.

88 Tilles, 2015, p131.

89 Tilles, 2015, p103.

90 Tilles, 2015, p141.

91 Tilles, 2015, p103.

92 Since 1841, the weekly *Jewish Chronicle* (JC) has regarded itself as the "organ of British Jewry", the national paper reporting on "Jewish affairs and news"; Rosenberg, 2011, p30.

93 Tilles, 2015, p102.

94 See Theodor Herzl's *Der Judenstaat (The Jewish State)*, written in 1896.

95 Barlow, Nigel, 2024, "Chaim Weizmann – The Manchester man behind the founding of Israel", aboutmanchester.co.uk

96 Williams, 1988, p29.

97 Simon Marks of the 'Marks & Spencer' retail giant.

98 Williams, 1988, p30.

99 Founded in 1911, *The Zionist Banner* was one of the first Zionist periodicals.

100 It was at the Seventh Zionist Congress held in July 1905 that "Uganda" was rejected; see *The Jewish Voice*, "Zionists' Seventh Congress", 4 August 1905; https://www.nli.org.il/en/newspapers/tjewvc/1905/08/04/01/page/3/?e=-------en-20--1--img-txIN%7CtxTI--------------1

101 Palestine has a three-thousand-year history that precedes the 1917 Balfour Declaration. See Krantz, 2019, "The long history of Palestine", *International Socialism* journal.

102 "As a result, shell production rose from 500,000 in the first five months of the First World War to 16.4 million in 1915", Barlow, 2024.

103 See Regan, Bernard, 2017, *The Balfour Declaration: Empire, the Mandate and Resistance in Palestine*, p55.

104 Tilles, 2015, p114.

105 Tilles, 2015, p114.

106 Tilles, 2015, p114.

107 Tilles, 2015, p125.

108 Tilles, 2015, p125.

109 Gewirtz, 1990, p25.

110 Tilles, 2015, p141.

Chapter 3
Building mass opposition to Mosley and the BUF

111 For a full list of YCL members, see, Crowley, Michael, 2022, *Comrades Come Rally! Manchester Communists in the 1930s and 1940s*, p319.

112 Williams, Bill, 2011, *Jews and Other Foreigners: Manchester and the Rescue of the Victims of European Fascism, 1933-1940*, p196.

113 Williams, 2011, p196.

114 Frow, Ruth and Frow, Edmund, 1978, *The Communist Party in Manchester, 1920-26*, p49.

115 Rothman, Benny, 2012, *The Battle for Kinder Scout: Including the 1932 Mass Trespass*.

116 Hann, Dave, 2013, *Physical Resistance: A Hundred Years of Anti-Fascism*, p53.

117 Reported in *The Blackshirt*, 25 January, 1935.

118 'Time and motion' was a system of monitoring work practices by managers intent on speeding up production and increasing the exploitation of workers.

119 Levine, 1984, p26.

120 Hann, 2013, p58.

Chapter 4
Communists, the Russian Revolution, and the United Front

121 See Sherry, Dave, 2017, *Russia 1917: Workers' Revolution and the Festival of the Oppressed*.

122 Trotsky, Leon, 1979, *History of the Russian Revolution*, pp711-728.

123 Cliff, Tony, 2000, *Marxism at the Millennium*, p60.

124 Hallas, Duncan, 1989, *The Comintern*, pp7-8.

125 See Trotsky, Leon, 1974, *The First Five Years of the Communist International*.

126 The quote is from Robert Brenner on the cover of Broué, Pierre, 2006, *The German Revolution 1917-23*.

127 Harman, 1982, from the book description on the back cover.

128 Harman, 1999, p479.

129 Stalin's policy was to promote the Anglo-Russian trade agreement. During the 1926 General Strike, CP members called for 'All power to the

General Council of the TUC'.
See Cliff and Gluckstein, 1986.

130 Stalin's policy was to pursue an 'alliance in the east'. Following the uprising of Chinese workers, Stalin's policy was to support the Chinese nationalist Chiang Kai-shek – who went on to butcher the communists and strangle the Chinese revolutionary movement. See Isaacs, Harold R., 1938, *The Tragedy of the Chinese Revolution*; Trotsky, Leon, *Leon Trotsky on China*, 1976.

131 Harman, 1999, p479. The 6th World Congress of the Comintern was held in Moscow, July 17-September 1, 1928. The sectarian policy introduced by Stalin known as the 'Third Period' lasted until 1933.

132 Stalin explained in 1931 the competitive dynamic that drove forced industrialisation at a cost of mass deprivation of the Russian people: "We are fifty or a hundred years behind the advanced countries. We must make good this lag in ten years. Either we do it, or they crush us." See Deutscher, Isaac, 1948, "The Economic Policy of the Soviet", *The Listener.*

133 Harman, 1999, p479.

134 Harman, 1999, p480.

135 Basketter, 2013.

136 Hallas, 1985, p103.

137 Sozialdemokratische Partei Deutschlands, the SPD.

138 Pearce, Brian and Woodhouse, Michael, 1995, *A History of Communism in Britain*, p195.

139 Pearce and Woodhouse, 1995, p195.

140 See Gluckstein, 1999, chapter 5, "The failure of the German left".

141 Led by Trotsky, the Left Opposition was the organised opposition to Stalin.

142 Groves, Reg, 1974, *The Balham Group: How British Trotskyism Began*, p65.

143 Bennett, Theresa, 2002, "The hidden history of Asians in Britain", *Socialist Worker.*

144 Groves, 1974, p75.

145 Groves, 1974, p75.

146 Pearce and Woodhouse, 1995, p211.

147 Pearce and Woodhouse, 1995, p212. In fact, as Pearce demonstrates, this was a faltering, uneven process. Nor did it involve any serious assessment of the disastrous consequences of the previous sectarian policy of the 'Third period' that had led to catastrophic defeat in Germany.

148 Pearce and Woodhouse, 1995, p214.

149 Pearce notes that even here "the content of these relations increasingly became reduced to a struggle by King Street [the CP's national headquarters] against 'Trotskyism' in the ILP".

150 Dorril, 2007, p231.

Chapter 5
1934: the fightback against Mosley begins

151 Forerunner to *The Guardian,* the *Manchester Guardian* was a daily paper, read nationally.

152 The first concentration camps were set up by the Spanish in Cuba, the British during the Boer War in South Africa, and the United States in the Philippines.

153 The Dachau camp was established to detain the "rapidly expanding number of political prisoners, most of them Social Democrats and Communists, arrested by the Nazis after the Reichstag Fire". As "the oldest and best-known *Konzentrationslager* (concentration camp) the Nazis readily granted tours of the camp to government functionaries, teachers, and students". By 1942 the Dachau concentration camp had become an "extermination camp, a death camp to murder and annihilate all races deemed 'degenerate'". See Dawsey, Jason, 2022, "Dachau, the 'Model' Concentration Camp, 1933-39", National World War 2 Museum.

154 *Manchester Guardian,* 1 January 1934.

155 Waterson, 2009.

156 The ILP was had been a constituent part of the Labour Party, but it disaffiliated in 1931; see Miliband,1972, p195. The ILP then moved to the left and, as "a left wing centrist organisation",

functioned as a propaganda group. Many ILP members joined anti-fascist protests. See Newsinger, John, 2023, "In the Middle of the Road: Fenner Brockway, the Independent Labour Party and the class struggle", *International Socialism* journal.

157 Walsh, David, 2011, "The Battle of Stockton", *Republic of Teesside* blog.

158 Serdiville, Rosie, 2018, "The Battle of Stockton Campaign", *North East History* 49.

159 Walsh, 2011.

160 Serdiville, 2018.

161 Hann, 2013, p30.

162 Hann, 2013, p31.

163 One in ten BUF members were women. The BUF wanted "men who were men, and women who were women". Men "dictated policy on birth control, sterilisation and abortion", Dorril, 2007, p227.

164 Hann, 2013, p31.

165 Rothman, 1994.

166 Tilles, 2015, p102.

167 Mullally, 1946, p30.

168 Dorril, 2007, p229; Hann, 2013, p28.

169 Tilles, 2015, p127.

170 Gewirtz, 1990, p25.

171 Todd, Nigel, 1995, *In Excited Times: The People Against the Blackshirts,* p56.

172 Todd, 1995, p56.

173 Todd, 1995, p58.

174 Maitles, Henry, 1994, "Blackshirts across the border", *Socialist Review;* O'Neill, Christina, 2019, "How Govanhill defeated Oswald Mosely's Blackshirts in the 1930s", *Glasgow Live.*

175 Mullally, 1946, p34.

176 Mullally, 1946, p34.

177 Mullally, 1946, p40.

178 Mullally, 1946, p35.

179 Dorril, 2007, p300.

180 O'Neill, 2014.

181 Jacobs, 1991, p144.

182 Jacobs, 1991, p145.

183 Dorril, 2007, p318.

184 Branson, 1985, p123; Jacobs, 1991, p145.

185 Jacobs, 1991, p144.

186 Jacobs, 1991, p144.

187 Waterson, 2009.

188 *Manchester Guardian*, 10 September 1934.

189 The leaflet detailed the crimes committed by the Nazi regime in the 8 months it had been in power, including: "3,000 put to death... 114,000 now in prisons and concentration camps, THAELMANN in prison 20 months without trial, suffering the most horrible torture." Ernst Thähmann was the leader of the German Communist Party. A copy of the leaflet is available at the People's History Museum.

190 *Manchester Guardian*, 18 September 1934.

191 The minutes of this Trades Council meeting were either 'lost' or destroyed.

192 This led in 1937 to the Labour Party Lord Mayor of Manchester, Leslie Lever, granting permission for the BUF to lease Cheetham Town Hall for a rally – on condition they abide by new legislation and did not wear their Blackshirts uniforms thus complying with the new Public Order Act which "banned political uniforms and gave extended powers to police to restrict processions", Rosenberg, 2011, p239.

193 See Manchester Watch Committee Reports, Book 186, 1934, available in the Cuttings archive in The People's History Museum.

194 Before the Belle Vue rally, Mosley had a short propaganda film made, 'Fiery speech in Manchester'. It was filmed indoors at a venue in Hulme, before the outdoor rally at Belle Vue. The film was not included in the cinema news clips of the time. This video of Mosley can be found on YouTube; https://www.youtube.com/watch?v=sPB1jy4vmFA

195 Hann, 2013, p58.

196 People's History Museum archive.

197 From the *Manchester Guardian* which carried extensive reports of the day.

198 These two songs are the two socialist anthems, the Labour

Party's *Red Flag*, and the Communist's *Internationale*.

199 The text of his antisemitic speech, not heard on the day, had been pre-released to the press ahead of the event.

200 Dorril, 2007, p320; Hann, 2013, p59.

201 Gray, Todd, 2006, *Blackshirts in Devon*, p52.

202 Gray, 2006, p54.

203 Gray, 2006, p67.

204 West Sussex Record Office, 2019, "Documenting Fascism in 1930s West Sussex".

205 Simkin, John, 2014, "The notorious Charles Bentinck Budd and the British Union of Fascists," *Sussex World.*

206 Simkin, 2014.

207 Simkin, 2014. Munich in south Germany had been a stronghold of Hitler's Nazi party.

208 Mosley is referring to what happened in September when 150,000 opposed the BUF in Hyde Park.

209 Hare, Chris, 1991, *Historic Worthing: The Untold Story*, p202.

210 Simkin, 2014.

211 Hare, 1991, p203.

212 Hare, 1991, p204.

213 Turner, David, 1993, *Fascism and Anti-Fascism in the Medway Towns, 1927-1940.*

Chapter 6
Halting the fascist momentum

214 Skidelsky, 1981, p331; Waterson, 2009.

215 Dorril, 2007, p349.

216 Dorril, 2007, p349.

217 Dorril, 2007, p349.

218 Dorril, 2007, p348.

219 Dorril, 2007, p350.

220 Høgsbjerg, Christian, 2006, "The fascist invasion of Abyssinia", *Socialist Worker.*

221 Kimber, Charlie, 2017, "A colonial massacre in Africa fully revealed for the first time", *Socialist Worker.*

222 Dorril, 2007, p360.

223 Dorril, 2007, p351.

224 The League of Nations was set up after the First World War promising to maintain a new era of peace. It was the forerunner of the United Nations.

225 Høgsbjerg, 2006.

226 Dorril, 2007, p368.

227 Høgsbjerg, 2006.

228 Dorril, 2007, p364.

229 Dorril, 2007, p368.

230 Mullally, 1946, p29.

231 *Manchester Guardian*, 18 September 1934.

232 Todd, 2006, p39.

233 Todd, 2006, p54.

234 Pike, Cecil, 1934, "British Union of Fascists", *Hansard*. Pike was an MP in Sheffield.

235 Turner, 1993.

236 Hann, 2013, p73.

237 Known as the July Agreement.

238 Hann, 2013, p73.

239 O'Neill, 2014.

240 Hann, 2013, p74.

241 Hann, 2013, p58.

242 *Daily Worker*, 22 September 1934.

243 Gewirtz, 1990, p25.

244 Dorril, 2007, p376.

245 Hann, 2013, p71. Mosley was speaking at Hulme Town Hall.

246 Young, Angus, 2017, "The Hull race riot involving flying bricks, razor blades in potatoes and a very controversial leader", *Hull Daily Mail*.

247 Young, 2017.

248 Flint, Josh, 2019, "Oswald Mosley and Leeds – The Battle of Holbeck Moor 27th September 1936", Leeds Libraries. See also, Burgon, Richard, 2024, "MP's Notebook: The Battle of Holbeck Moor", *South Leeds Life*.

249 Hann, 2013, p74.

250 Flint, 2019.

251 Rosenberg, 2011, p193.

252 Newsinger, 2023.

253 Rosenberg, 2011, p196.

254 Jacobs, 1991, p237.

255 Sparks, Colin, 1978-79, "Masses against Mosley", *Socialist Review*

no. 8, pp24-25.

256 Sparks, Colin, 1977, "Fighting the Beast: Fascism – The Lessons of Cable Street", *International Socialism* journal

257 Jacobs, 1991, p241.

258 Jacobs, 1991, p241.

259 Newsinger, 2023, p150; Rosenberg, 2011, p196.

260 Jacobs, 1991, p242.

261 Rosenberg, 2011, p202; Independent Labour Party, 1936, *They Did NOT Pass: 300,000 workers Say NO To Mosley*.

262 Independent Labour Party, 1936.

263 Rosenberg, 2011, p204.

264 Piratin, 1948, p24.

265 Piratin, 1948, p24.

266 Independent Labour Party, 1936.

267 Dorril, p395; Rosenberg, 2011, p216.

268 *Fighting Talk*, 1996.

269 *Fighting Talk*, 1996.

270 *Fighting Talk*, 1996.

Chapter 7
Blackshirt Bye Bye

271 Waterson, 2009.

272 Duncan Hallas summed up Trotsky's assessment of Stalin's political zig zags: "swinging right (1923), left (1924), right (1925-27), left (1928-33), right (1934) and finally ending up on the side of the bourgeois order (in

its 'democratic' form) from 1935 onwards", see Hallas, Duncan, [1951], "The Stalinist Parties" reprinted in Hallas and others, 2023, *Indomitable Revolutionary*, p67. More zig zags followed the Popular Front policy. The years of 'opposing Nazi aggression' ended in 1939 when Stalin agreed to a non-aggression pact with Hitler. After Hitler invaded Russia in 1941, Stalin reversed position yet again, "to give uncritical support for Churchill's Coalition and the war effort"; see Sherry, 2023, p262.

273 Harman, Chris, 1999, *A People's History of the World*, p494.

274 Harman, 1999, p494.

275 Harman, 1999, p494.

276 Harman, 1999, p495.

277 Danos, Jacques, and Gibelin, Marcel, 1986, *June '36: Class Struggle and the Popular Front in France*, p34.

278 Danos and Gibelin, 1986, p109.

279 Cliff, Tony, 1993, *Trotsky 1927–40: The Darker the Night the Brighter the Star*, p193.

280 The Franco-Soviet Treaty of Mutual Assistance.

281 Harman, 1999, p499.

282 Newsinger, John, 2018, *Hope Lies in the Proles: George Orwell and the Left*, p15.

283 A total of 335,000 men and women from around the world volunteered to fight against Franco's forces. See Tremlett, Giles, 2021, *The International Brigades: Fascism, Freedom and the*

Spanish Civil War.

Chapter 8
Anti-fascists after Cable Street

284 Córdoba is a town in the Spanish State.

285 Levine, 1984, p30.

286 O'Riordan, Manus, 2008, "George Brown and the Defence of the Spanish Republic", https://lbocanegra.eu/?p=102&sez=bi#rior

287 See Jones, Jack, 1986, *Union Man: Autobiography*.

288 The ILP organised some International Brigades, most however were controlled by the Communist Party.

289 Basketter, 2020.

290 Newsinger, 2018, p15.

291 Eric Arthur Blair (George Orwell) was in Spain with his wife Eileen Maud Blair (nee, Eileen O'Shaughnessy).

292 Partido Obrero de Unificación Marxista (Workers' Party of Marxist Unification) was an anti-Stalinist party which represented the radical or left wing in the struggle against fascism during the Spanish Civil War.

293 Funder, Anna, 2023, *Wifedom: Mrs Orwell's Invisible Life*, pp115-120.

294 Newsinger, 2018, p16.

295 For contemporary debates over

Popular Front and united front strategies, see Callinicos, Alex, 2021 "Neoliberal capitalism implodes: global catastrophe and the far right today", *International Socialism* journal.

296 See Ali, 2022, pp183-190.

297 Fyrth, Jim (ed.), 1985, *British Fascism and the Popular Front,* p23.

298 After Cable Street, it was the ILP, not the CP, that rushed out a celebratory pamphlet, *They Did NOT pass: 300,000 Workers Say NO to Mosley*; see Rosenberg, 2011, p202. For an example of the omission by the CP over its involvement in opposing Mosley, see Pollitt, Harry, 1940, *Serving My Time: An Apprenticeship to Politics.*

299 Clinch, Dave 2006, "Left History: Rising from the East", *Socialist Review.*

300 Piratin, preface to the 1978 edition, pvii.

301 Rosenberg, 2011, p160.

302 In France in 2023 workers engaged in a series of general strikes and mass demonstrations, but in the absence of a mass anti-fascist movement directly targeting Rassemblement National, support for the fascist Marine Le Pen has not been broken.

303 Piratin, 1948, p17.

304 Jacobs, 1991, p151.

305 After Cable Street "the BUF East End campaign saw an increase in attacks on Jews by young fascist hooligans. The breaking of shop windows, the desecration of Jewish cemeteries and synagogues", Dorril, 2007, p395. The "public abuse of Jewry remained strong and continued to be disseminated", Rosenberg, 2011, p244. In 1945 Mosley held a series of street meetings in London proclaiming, "not enough Jews were burned at Belsen" death camp, demanding, "Get rid of the Jews! and Burn the synagogues!"; Beckman, Morris, 2013, *The 43 Group: Battling Mosley's Blackshirts,* p33. A group of Jewish ex-servicemen formed the 43 Group to organise confrontation with Mosley's fascists. The CP, with its Popular Front policy, did not join these anti-fascist protests.

306 Beckman, Morris, 2018, "Fighting fascists: Battling Oswald Mosley's Blackshirts", thehistorypress.co.uk

307 Hayes, Ali, 2019, "The day Oswald Mosley spoke to 15,000 people at Southampton Common – and was hit by a rock", *Southern Daily Echo.*

308 Boisseau, Will, 2011, "Remembering and Forgetting Anti-Fascism", *History Workshop Journal.*

309 Hayes, 2019.

310 Boisseau, 2011.

311 *Fighting Talk,* 1996

312 mudlark121, 2019, "Today in London anti-fascist history, 1937: mass opposition prevents British Union of Fascists marching into Bermondsey", *London Radical Histories.*

313 Rosemberg, David, 2019, "On
   this day – 3 October 1937:
   the battle of Bermondsey",
   rebellion602.wordpress.com

314 mudlark121, 2019. The local
   Labour Party opposed the
   counter-demonstration, but many
   Labour Party members took part.

315 mudlark 121, 2019.

316 The CP Historians Group was
   set up in 1951.

317 Ashman, Sam, 1998, "The
   Communist Party Historians
   Group" in Rees, John (ed.), *Essays
   on Historical Materialism.*

318 Ashman, 1998, p146.

319 Ashman, 1998, p148.

320 Ashman, 1998, p148.

321 Trotsky, 1979, p17.

322 In Moscow, Stalin set up a
   series of "show trials which
   sentenced people to execution
   or the living death of labour
   camps… The depiction of the
   accused as 'Trotskyist foreign
   agents' deflected mass bitterness
   away from the regime towards
   alleged 'saboteurs'. The climax of
   the terror in 1936-37 involved
   the condemning to death of
   all of the remaining members
   of Lenin's central committee
   of 1917, except for Stalin,
   Alexandra Kollontai… and Leon
   Trotsky, who survived in exile, to
   be assassinated by Stalin's agents
   in 1940"; Harman, 1999, p477.